TRANSFORMING

the believer

TRANSFORMING

the believer

Jerry S. Eicher

WINEPRESS **WP** PUBLISHING

Contents

Introduction

This is a story at once of bread making, a quite natural process, and the greater spiritual story of how a man or a woman is made into the image of God. In an instant age, we often have forgotten that the completed works of God are not done in a moment of time. Even our conversion, which we often remember only as the moment of decision, was really an experience stretching over a period of time in which God pursued us unto Himself. So much more the transformation into the image of God is itself a long journey. Let us have the courage to travel the road.

PART ONE—

THE MAKING OF THE BREAD

The Body

1

On the night that He was betrayed, the Son of Man, who was the Saviour of the World, took bread in His hands, blessed it, broke it, and gave to His disciples to eat. "Take eat," He said, "For this is my body" (Mark 14:22). Common bread, made with common hands, was that night exalted, to represent the Living Bread that came down, and still comes down, from heaven. The Son of Man could have chosen the delicate food prepared by trained hands and served in kings' homes—food that entices those already satiated. But He passed up that for food eaten by the hungry—ordinary, satisfying bread.

There in Jerusalem that night, He held in His hands the representation of the miracle of life. A common food, prepared daily in a thousand households, would come to represent the awe of heavenly movements. Life had begun in a stable, amid straw and oxen and sheep. So life would go on now—born not in the halls of the mighty or the religious, but in the humble hearts of men and women who would tremble with the knowledge that they are held in the hands of God.

The Body, the Church of the Living God, would be formed as a miracle. Not a miracle contained in the assembling of the ingredients, but a miracle contained in the ingredients themselves. Two or three people would be the assembly. This gift would be given to them, and though a multitude copy the pattern, such life would never come to pass without a miracle.

"*This is my body.*" The Church, the Body of Christ, is grounded on this miracle. But there is no ground perhaps harder to hold or more fiercely contested. Many thinkers have developed doctrines of the Body, but thought or theological positions do not conceive a body. The Body is a miracle. Its conception is a miracle, its birth is a miracle, its growth is a miracle, and its life is a miracle.

That's not to say the Body is mystical or unattainable. Nothing is more basic to our existence. The bread in His hands showed us that. The bread was not proud, as the Body is not proud. The bread itself was the identity, as the Body itself is the identity, not its doctrines or theological positions. A humble and broken people are the ones who can be made into a Body.

The Body has many different parts that together manifest the Holy Spirit, who gives us the parts. The apostle Paul understood the context of the manifestations to be first and foremost local. It is quite easy to get along with and appreciate the gifts of someone a hundred miles away, but it's a far more rigorous process to function with people we live with day by day. With those we find the practical application of being made into children of God.

In fellowship there is an equality of value, not an equality of function. The apostle Paul calls this recognition of value "*honour*" (1 Cor. 12:23). The cross has come to bring an end to competitiveness and concerns about who is greatest among us. Without the cross there is no fellowship. Fellowship is where people of completely different functions live in peace with each other. The world seeks to make people similar and equal in order to obtain peace, but the Church embraces people of great differences, for all enmity has been slain by the cross (Eph. 2:15–16). So it is that fellowship is a concept unique to the New Testament. Here all that is born of the Spirit is given its place. Not a place to be equal in function, but a place for all to be; for it is the place, not the function that gives the value. For now it is no more the individual but the many that are the one man in Christ.

If God will bring life to the Body, the Body will bring life to the world. By and large that's *not* the kind of living church we have in Christianity. What with projects, theological positions, meetings, and programs, the miracle of life is lost. Christianity is not simply many carbon copies of a single theological school or thought. If you have seen one, as they say, you have seen them all. The true Body is not that way. No man is complete in himself, nor is any revelation or train of religious thought. It is the Body of Christ that is whole, as made clear in Scripture. Weirdness and carbon copies are both unscriptural. Deadness makes for sameness. What is alive is different.

The unity is contained in the life. The nose is as different from the hand in the same body as you can make it because both are alive. The foot is as different from the skin in the same body as you can make it because both are alive. Such is the work of God's hands. Men try to have church, but it cannot be done without a miracle. The works of man are complicated, but the assembly of the miracle is simple. As simple as bread. That night Jesus held the representation in His hands, as He would hold all those who are birthed of the Spirit in His hands. So Christ forever took life out of the hands of the religious rich with their theological thoughts and schools, and placed life in the rough-hewn hands of the humble and broken in spirit.

That that bread should still feed the world is indeed not a marvel to the hungry. They desire to be filled with wholesome food. The same is true of the spiritually hungry. Christ laid on the table the simple, unadorned Word of God. The manna from heaven still lies outside the tent on the ground, lowly, humble, making no claims to its owns greatness, "a small round thing as small as the hoar frost on the ground" (Exod. 16:4).

Truth on this earth is still served plain. Pride drives us to serve food that makes the server look good. But the hungry care nothing about the pride of the server, and enjoy holding and tasting the bread itself. Let the exalted worry about exaltation; it is the hungry that will be filled with good things.

Jesus said, *"I am the bread that came down from heaven"* (John 6:41). So now His Church shall become "bread," that in each generation life might be manifested to the world. Much of today's food is but stale, moldy bread served from textbooks and history references. The cross stands here also, so that each generation of the Church can be born again and eat anew the life-giving Bread of heaven. The apostle Paul speaks of the offense of the cross that cuts across all human experience when dealing with the divine. Our bread may be for our children and their children to eat, but it is not for them to serve. Bread must be made fresh in them again. God will have bread.

The Harvest

2

God makes His "bread" as man makes his, from the grain of the harvest. Man has a harvest each year, just as God has a harvest in each generation. God's harvest involves not just bringing in souls, but also righteousness that grows in the heart. Out of the harvest comes the wheat used to make bread. When there is no more harvest, there can be no more bread.

Jesus said, "*Except a corn of wheat fall into the ground and die, it abideth alone. . . .*" (John 12:24). There is a life that comes from heaven, which is not from this world. "*For he shall grow up before him as a tender plant, and as a root out of a dry ground. . . .*" (Isa. 53:2).

Our world knows of tender plants and of fertile roots, but not of growing out of dry ground. Such was prophesied of the seed of Christ. There would be a seed come into our world that would grow, full and blooming, and do so in the desert. Not because it was watered and kept in the desert, but because it had *life in itself.* Christ took no nutrients from our soil. He came with another life that needed no strength from the soil of this world. Here He blossomed as a rose.

The religious grow things by force out of the ground of the desert, which appeals to us greatly. If it is birthed of this earth it must be force-grown, for the desert produces little food on its own. Heaven has come with a seed that grows in the desert, without our normal methods of growth. This life grows from a source other than work, sweat, and pressure.

It is not that the religious can grow no crop in the desert. They can. It is that heaven rejects the product. From the seed of man grows the sufficient quantity, but not the quality, to make bread. Great is the neglect in not dividing that which is born from God from that which is born of the earth. You get apostasy from the wrong seed.

Christ still says what He told Nicodemus that night, *"Except a man be born again, he cannot see the kingdom of God. . . . That which is born of the flesh is flesh; and that which is born of the Spirit is spirit"* (John 3:3, 6).

In this matter of the harvest, how can we proceed further until we are certain what we are dealing with? Men's opinions are by the millions and books by the thousands, but what is born of God? Men ask that question only when it is too late to find the answer. It is in the dawning of a thing, in its birthing, that we must pause and ask, "Whose son are you?" Men have skirted the altar where things can be dealt with in their infancy, and only when the sun is high do they ask whether what they have, has been birthed of God. A barley field when half-grown is no time to inquire of the origins of the seed.

Men generally settle for growth and success, and measure their lives accordingly. Heaven doesn't argue with our joy at success and growth, for heaven itself abounds with success and growth, but it argues with where we got our seed, for there is a great difference. It matters of what sort it is. It matters very much.

THE LAW OF THE HARVEST

The right seed can't just sit in the ground, however. There must be a harvest. The farmer plants his seeds, spends all that money, and puts in all that time and trouble, not just so he can sleep well at night thinking about his nice seeds. He plants them for the joy of the harvest. So God plants expecting that His word will not come back to Him void (Isa. 55:11).

There would be little joy in nice green plants in nice straight rows, well weeded, and well fertilized, if there was no hope of a harvest. No farmer grows the field for the memories; he grows the field for the harvest. If the harvest fails he has failed. If the harvest fails, it doesn't matter how the field looked or how well he plowed. If the harvest fails, it doesn't matter who had the best leaves. If the harvest fails, then things have failed.

God's harvest is not limited to bringing in souls. The harvest involves holy things, birthed of God deep within our hearts. Out of breaking and plowing in our lives, the giving of His mercy and the plying of His Word grows a harvest. Righteousness grows and bears life in the believer. As men gather from their gardens, so also God gathers from His.

Repentance is the ground from which the harvest is born. The church or man that has forsaken an intimate, personal relationship of repentance with God has no harvest. For there is no other ground out of which the heavenly seed grows. It is from the place of weeping that we return with joy, bearing the sheaves with us (Ps. 126:6).

THE UNPREPARED GROUNDS

"Behold, a sower went forth to sow; And when he sowed, some seeds fell by the way side, and the fowls came and devoured them up: Some fell upon stony places, where they had not much earth: and forthwith they sprung up, because they had no deepness of earth: And when the sun was up, they were scorched; and because they had no root, they withered away. And some fell among thorns; and the thorns sprung up, and choked them: But other fell into good ground, and brought forth fruit, some an hundredfold, some sixtyfold, some thirtyfold. Who hath ears to hear, let him hear." (Matt. 13:3–9)

In interpreting this Scripture, we generally categorize people into permanent states of hard ground, stony ground, thorny ground, or good ground. This interpretation suggests that the hard ground in not workable, the stony ground is useless, the thorny ground is hopeless, and only the good ground is of any use. Good ground is acquired by some mysterious means, but speakers assume all their listeners have it, for no one wants to call his audience a hopeless situation. We are left with but one option of workability; that is, good ground. All the other grounds must apply to someone else.

This interpretation cannot be correct, for if all of us are good ground, we would need no further working. Good ground is already good and should produce a great harvest. We must look to a more practical interpretation that has meaning for all of us: God is able to take any of these grounds by His grace and work them into productive grounds. No ground is considered hopeless ground. Isn't the sower casting seed upon all the grounds? No farmer would waste seed on hopeless ground, and neither would God.

THE WAYSIDE

The hard ground is the ground of the wayside, a well-traveled ground. The Scriptures say ". . . it was trodden down . . ." (Luke 8:5). All who wish to might pass over the wayside: the cart and the chariot, the horse and the automobile, the man and the beast are equally welcome on its road. Be it left or right, conservative or liberal, there is no stopping its traffic; it remains free and open. Seed cast upon this ground has no dirt and darkness of the soil to hide it, and so the fowls of the air carry it away. This is ground unbroken and unfenced and unrestricted.

There are men who pride themselves in the seclusion of their doctrinal niche, but they are not really alone with God. In the vast regions of such a man's heart the silent testimony is borne as the rain falls and the sun shines and the seed is sown, but there is not even the sprouting, let alone the harvest which is borne in the presence of the Father.

The answer in the natural world, as well as in the spiritual, is to reclaim the ground. It must be fenced in and the way shut off to traffic. If you want righteousness to grow in the heart of the Church, you cannot let just anything run over the land. Seed is planted alone in the dark of the soil. There it must have quietness, peace, and darkness. Things are what they are. If we will grow holy things in the home or the church, there must be fathers and leaders there who have the courage to put up a fence and stand at the gate to keep out what is running over the field and preventing a harvest.

We have psychologists and psychiatrists, licensed and unlicensed, in and out of church. We have teachers and opinions and doctrines. We have scares and crises and the latest religious movements. We have thoughts about this and thoughts about that, and tongues running everywhere and wonder why our ground is unproductive and unbroken.

The ground to be productive must be fenced off. The fence offends people. The fence makes trouble. The fence stops the traffic. With the traffic stopped, the rain and the wind can soften the ground so the plow will take hold. Good ground is limited ground.

People and the neighbors will say, "Didn't he grow up among us, and don't we know him? Who does he think he is?" Such a man does not think he is anything, he is just trying to have a harvest.

Stony Ground

Then there is the stony ground. Rocks are just everywhere. Offenses, misunderstandings, feelings, hurts, and bitterness are all there. Things between brother and brother, a man and his wife, business deals gone badly. Even God says, "Behold I lay in Zion a stumbling stone and a rock of offense. . . ." (Rom. 9:33). That is just the way it is. To have our own way opposed creates offense.

There is One who came from heaven who was "despised and rejected of men; a man of sorrows, and acquainted with grief: and we hid as it were our faces from him; he was despised, and we esteemed him not. Surely he hath borne our griefs, and carried our sorrows: yet we did esteem him stricken, smitten of God, and afflicted. But he was wounded for our transgressions, he was bruised for our iniquities, the chastisement of our peace was upon him; and with his stripes we are healed" (Isa. 53:3–5).

This world has rocks in it, plenty of them everywhere, and most people do too—hard experiences, rough places, hurts, and feelings that have hardened us. The devil told Jesus to turn stones into bread (Luke 4:3). The devil is still saying that, and sadly some of the Church listens. Jesus refused to use stones to make bread, and still does. You cannot use your hard experiences to make something good to eat. Your stones must be ground to powder. There before your very eyes must something be destroyed that you had hoped would at least be of some use after all the pain you went through. It must be mixed in with the soil of your life, out of your control, but in the control of God, to grow out of the soil what God desires.

2 Corinthians 5:17: "Therefore if any man be in Christ, he is a new creature: old things are passed away; behold, all things are become new."

The Church doesn't need the psychiatrist's couch. Calvary has the answer. Love is not avoiding the problem or covering it up, but love is the breaking up of the stones.

The apostle Paul shook off his offense into the fire. While the rest of the people present waited for him to die, he shook off the snake into the fire and was unharmed. When deadly things happen to men and women, the world sees no way of survival. But there was One who died so I can live; there was One who bore my stripes so I can be healed. These offenses, these wounds, were answered at Calvary by One who came to bring us the life of another.

The husbandman comes quickly so he might deal with all that hinders his harvest. The cross calls to all as an answer to that which offends: if we will die, we shall live. The

Scriptures say, "and nothing shall offend them" (Ps. 119:165).

THORNY GROUND

Then there is the thorny ground. No examination under a microscope is necessary—we have just plain old "thorns": the cares of this world, the need to find a job, the need to take care of a family, the need to make money, a sick child, my position at work, advancement at the company, cold, heat, rain, and snow. In any of these concerns can grow a thorn bush that chokes out the plant God planted. If we are to have a harvest, the thorn bush must be pulled up. We will always have problems; it is the care that grows out of them that must be uprooted.

Jesus said, "Take no thought for your life, what ye shall eat, or what ye shall drink; nor yet for your body, what ye shall put on. Is not the life more than meat, and the body than raiment? Behold the fowls of the air; for they sow not, neither do they reap, nor gather into barns; yet your heavenly Father feedeth them. Are ye not much better than they? Which of you by taking thought can add one cubit unto his stature? And why take ye thought for raiment? Consider the lilies of the field, how they grow; they toil not, neither do they spin: And yet I say unto you, That even Solomon in all his glory was not arrayed like one of these. Wherefore, if God so clothe the grass of the field, which today is, and tomorrow is cast into the oven, shall he not much more clothe you, O ye of little faith? Therefore take no thought, saying, What shall we eat? Or, What shall we drink? Or Wherewithal shall we be clothed? For after all these things do the Gentiles seek: for your heavenly Father knoweth that ye have need of all these things. But seek ye first the kingdom of God, and his righteousness; and all these things shall be added unto you." (Matt. 6:25–33)

Only those with faith in the love and care of the Father—who pulls the cares from our lives—will bear a harvest. The love of the Father is not a matter just for children that the rest of us outgrow. It is one of the greatest truths of the Bible, and as is the case with first things, it will be there at the end.

THE TARES

"Another parable put He forth unto them saying, The kingdom of heaven is likened unto a man which sowed good seed in his field. And while men slept his enemy came and sowed tares among the wheat, and went his way. . . . Let both grow together until the harvest: and in the time of the harvest I will say to the reapers, Gather ye together first the tares, and bind them in bundles to burn them: but gather the wheat into my barn." (Matt. 13:24–25, 30)

Out of this Scripture comes our understanding of the tares. We learn what is done at harvests. The harvest spoken of here is the end of the world, when all tares will be brought to an end. While our harvest is not the end of the world, we still must separate the tares from the wheat in order to make bread. There must be no tares in the bread, for they are poisonous. The grains of the tares, if eaten, will produce convulsions and even death.

Tares are a concern in every ground that seeks to have a harvest. According to this Scripture, the enemy comes while men sleep and sows his own seed, which when sprouting will look like the wheat. In a moment of inattention this seed of the enemy is sown.

This weed was called *darnel* and looks very much like wheat before it comes into ear. Hence, the command that the tares should be left until the harvest, lest while men plucked up the tares they also should root up the wheat. These stalks of tares would be inseparable from the wheat, because prior to the harvest they were hardly distinguishable from the wheat. The closest scrutiny would often fail to detect them. Farmers in those days, who generally weeded their fields, would not attempt to separate the darnel from the wheat before the harvest. In the time of the harvest they could be separated. When the wind blew across the field of grain ripe for harvest, the wheat, having substance, bowed, but the tares, lacking substance, did not bow. They were then easily distinguishable.

There is a time when this weed can be separated from the wheat. Men of God who lead the church must in times of harvest mark well what is revealed and not allow tares to be gathered into the bread. Men and women who look right, sound right, think right, hold right doctrines, and work in right denominations may yet be tares that defile and poison—birthed by another seed sown by the enemy. Pastors gather members into the church on many standards designed to keep out stones, thorns, and hard ground. Yet none of these standards will keep out tares.

There is but one ground on which to distinguish tares and wheat, and those are the grounds of the harvest. It is the church with a present visitation and voice from heaven that has the ability to make pure bread, and that church only. What does not bow in the voice and wind of God must not be gathered into the church, no matter how good it looks. It may have the most money, the best looks, and the greatest range of talents, but if it cannot bow in the harvest, it is a tare.

People will want to know why you left such a thing in the field. The testimony of the man was so great and his gift so usable. But as the Scriptures say, man looks on the outward appearance, but God looks on the heart.

Tares also may be ideas or dreams that grow within a believer's life. That splendid idea that seems so inspired may indeed be inspired, but by the wrong source. Even the disciple Peter had to be rebuked by Jesus for allowing the devil to speak through him when the subject of the crucifixion came up. Before the wind that blew by the Spirit of God, Peter's ideas found no ability to bow, and Jesus said, "*Get thee behind me Satan*" (Mark 8:33).

The Threshing Floor

3

From the harvest the sheaves are taken to the threshing floor. Teaching in the Church functions as the threshing floor, providing believers a way to remove chaff from their lives. Many believers don't belong to a church such as that, and so are not totally to blame for their condition. They are born again and desire the will of God but have no tools for further growth in their Christian lives.

Much of the Christian experience in today's churches leads up to this point in bread making and stops. The Christian life is limited to becoming born again and then turning around and leading other people to be born again. Individuals don't deal with the chaff, either in their own lives, or in the lives of others. So the Christian experience is one of striving to win a fresh harvest, losing the current harvest in the process.

The farmer doesn't know what to do with sheaves except thresh them, and neither should the Church. In churches that do not have a threshing ministry, people tend to sit around and simply look at the sheaves. The only occupation they seem concerned about is soul winning. When sheaves are sent out to sow the next harvest, many naturally sow, through no fault of their own, what they have to sow, which is their own seeds and chaff. The seeds from the sheaves were not intended for sowing but for bread making. Sowing your own seeds creates problems, and your chaff produces nothing, except perhaps disillusionment for those who place their faith in it.

The result is a lot of activity with few results, and what does grow is often illegitimate, as we are commanded to use seeds from heaven and not our own. Jesus said, *"Believest thou not that I am in the Father, and the Father in me? the words that I speak unto you I speak not of myself: but the Father that dwelleth in me, he doeth the works"* (John 14:10). The correct method of the harvest is found in Psalms. There a man goes forth bearing precious seed, not his own seed, weeping, and returns rejoicing with sheaves. *"He that goeth forth and weepeth, bearing precious seed, shall doubtless come again with rejoicing, bringing his sheaves with him"* (Ps. 126:6).

Sheaves containing both wheat and chaff are then intended to be brought into a gathering of believers who have a threshing floor, there to be threshed. Each man's life that is born of God contains both wheat and chaff. The wheat is birthed within the chaff, both from the seed of God. For bread to be made, the one must be separated from the other. Sheaves left to themselves can contain some good, for sheaves do contain wheat, but bread cannot be made except by threshing the wheat from the chaff.

Many ministries and people seek to function and produce only with sheaves. The reasons are many, but the results are much the same: if it is soul winning, confusion, and disillusionment; if it is an attempt at bread making, it is bread that goes further but does not satisfy. Again disillusionment and confusion may set in. Who is satisfied to chew on chaff for any length of time?

The reason we see so little purity in the people of God is that so little chaff is ever removed. God intends that chaff be removed from the life of believers. That is the heart of the mission and purpose of the local church. It is here that men and women can be changed into the image of the Son of God from glory to glory (2 Cor. 3:18).

Churches who have as their theme *"Go ye into all the world, and preach the gospel to every creature"* (Mark 16:15) may get high marks for zeal but have misunderstood their rightful mission. Evangelism is not the primary focus of the Church's existence. God has set many offices and gifts in the Church, of which the evangelist is only one. These offices and gifts are to edify the Body (Eph. 4:11–12). The purpose of the local church is to make "bread," which will edify the world, but to become bread, the believer himself must be edified.

If anything ranks among the great problems of this world, it is the obfuscation of believers of their position as the recipients of the blessings of God. God's blessings are not what the world counts as blessings, such as riches and fame, but spiritual success and growth. To be blessed is not only to be conformed to the likeness of the death of Christ, but also to the likeness of his resurrection (Rom. 6:5). Threshing fosters the growth and purification that makes us more and more like the risen Christ in all His glory.

One reason we fail to invest time and effort in the threshing ministry may be our desire to produce what wins the applause of the moment. Threshing requires time and patience. Jesus left at age twelve what seemed to be a quite fruitful ministry to return home with His parents, and as a result, increased in wisdom and stature and in favor with God and man (Luke 2:49–52). Much of the running to and fro, with activities of the Church, only draw us away from edification, proving a hindrance to the work of God. The upkeep of meetings, laws, religious systems and orders often only drains a believer who would be conformed to the image of God.

Hiding Instead of Threshing

Our human nature tries to hide our weaknesses. God's way is to expose them. There ought to be one place on this earth where a person can be honest about who he is without fear. God has ordained that place to be among believers. Jesus said, "A new commandment I give unto you, That ye love one another; as I have loved you, that ye also love one another" (John 13:34). Few things perhaps testify as much to the lack of love in the Church as the fear of harm because of honesty. Where there is love a believer can be real. *"Hatred stirreth up strifes: but love covereth all sins"* (Prov. 10:12).

To have to be afraid to be honest in church is to make a mockery of the very heart and purpose of the existence of the Church. Honesty may in fact be safer in many bars and street corners of the world than in many churches. We hinder the work of God when we pretend that all is wheat, when it really is not. Some say that because we are born again, all must be wheat. But the new birth experience does not remove the need for sanctification. Is not sanctification for believers (1 Thess. 4:1–4)? We are to bring the sheaves into the church. Unrefined, unpolished, itchy though they may be, they must be brought into the church and placed on the threshing floor. Some local assemblies have a cleaning-up class, a how-to-talk-the-doctrine class, for newly born-again souls before they allow them in, while the scriptural method is to accept them in for further sanctification by the function of the Body itself.

Jesus said in Matthew 23:28, "*Even so ye also outwardly appear righteous unto men, but within ye are full of hypocrisy and iniquity.*" Hypocrisy feels at home in religious circles, because most religion is about hiding what we are. Christianity is about exposing it, not to the world or to prying eyes, but where it is safe so we can be rid of what is wrong. The church that is afraid to thresh is afraid to be the Church.

The threshing floor was usually placed on a high place such as a tall hill or plateau where it was windy. Wind was needed to blow away the chaff. Jesus said, "*A city that is set on an hill cannot be hid*" (Matt. 5:14). On a hill everyone can see what you are doing and what is going on as far as whether we are threshing or not. You could place the threshing floor down in the valley where it could be hid, but where is the wind to blow away the chaff? The Church must get up on the hill to do its work, and the work is to thresh.

A church threshing on a hilltop comes to the light, and while walking in that light, becomes itself the light. Here good works are done for the world to see and glorify the Father in heaven. But in reality most unbelievers know that more hiding goes on in churches than exposing, and they do not glorify the Father in heaven.

Matthew 5:14–16: "*Ye are the light of the world. A city that is set on an hill cannot be hid. Neither do men light a candle, and put it under a bushel, but on a candlestick; and it giveth light unto all that are in the house. Let your light so shine before men, that they may see your good works, and glorify your Father which is in heaven.*"

The world wants to see the works of God. Seekers from the world are not looking primarily for a fasting church, a praying church, or a missionary-minded church. They are looking to see whether such a place can change men and women. This is the work of God, to change things from how they are to how they ought to be.

Those who walk in the world know the world holds no power to really change men. Riches, power, position, drink—all offer that promise but hold no such power. Does the Church hold such a power? On the answer hangs more than you may think.

Sheaves are brought to the threshing floor that the chaff might be gotten out of them. Here on the threshing floor the old oxen trod around and around. In third world countries this method is still used. Oxen are tied to the end of a long pole that is fastened by the other end to a rotating center. The sheaves are laid for the oxen to walk on and thresh.

As an allegory, the oxen are the ministry of the Church—around and around, meeting after meeting, treading out the sheaves. Oxen don't care where they put their feet down; it is not a personal matter with them. Chaff or wheat, they just step on everything, treading out the corn. So in the Church—if it is personal it is not threshing. Threshing is impersonal, separating you from the chaff in your life. Your nice testimonies, great works, deep conversions, stepping on it all. This is the work of the Church. Working on the harvest of God. Things that were prayed for, things fasted for, things travailed for, treading upon it all on the threshing floor, working out the chaff. Working everything loose from the wheat, for that is what the Master wants to make bread with. Sheaves birthed of heaven, and the preacher just walks all over it. This is the work of God.

The failure of men to thresh may well be one of the reasons behind Isaiah 63:1–6: "Who is this that cometh from Edom, with dyed garments. . . . Wherefore art thou red in thine apparel, and thy garments like him that treadeth in the winevat? I have trodden the winepress alone; and of the people there was none with me: for I will tread them in mine anger, and trample them in my fury; . . . And I looked, and there was none to help; and I wondered that there was none to uphold: therefore mine own arm brought salvation unto me; and my fury, it upheld me. And I will tread down the people in mine anger."

Further Growth 4

The Winnowing

Then there is winnowing. Matthew 3:12: "*Whose fan is in his hand, and he will thoroughly purge his floor.*" Winnowing was not done with a shovel but with a fork-like instrument that had prongs on it. The fork was stuck underneath the whole pile and everything thrown up into the air. On the hilltop, with the wind blowing, the chaff would catch the wind and blow over the hillside, but the heavier wheat would fall back again onto the threshing floor. This was the process. Send the ox around for awhile, stick in the fork, throw it up. Such is the threshing ministry of the Church. Things you thought were tremendous, all gone over the hillside. But in the meantime, that which is real, the substance, the wheat, is finding its place back down on the threshing floor, back on the rock at the feet of the winnower. To be found as wheat is to find ourselves again at the feet of Jesus. It is the substance that keeps coming back down. If it goes over the hill, let it go. If the wind can catch it, then let it catch it. It is not worth having. No matter how long you have prayed over it, no matter how long you have fasted over it, no matter how much you love it, if it can be blown, let it blow, because what God is after is the "real," that which is alive in you.

It is a tragedy when the wheat will not separate from the chaff. If the kernel will not break, it is possible that the wind will catch both chaff and wheat and blow them both over the hillside. Breaking and breaking and breaking are necessary for threshing. Even in those churches that avoid threshing, the principles of God cannot be avoided, and when the winds blow, many that are not broken blow away.

Sifting

From the threshing floor everything that has substance is picked up and taken to be sifted. What has substance is not all wheat. Gravel, rocks, or other debris also may have been picked up and must now be taken out, lest someone crack his tooth on it. "Unsifted" Christian men and women have in them what is hard and unbreakable.

We must discern between stable and hard, stubborn and workable, but who is equal to such judging? Failure must judge. Sifting is failure. Failure is a necessary part of bread making. God is more concerned about the rocks in your life than about how bad your failure looks. To sift the wheat the farmer would pour it through a screen or wire type mesh that would keep the rocks and debris on top, so they could be thrown away. There is much hardness in many Christian people that needs to be thrown away. Failure allows this to be done without losing the wheat. Many preachers will preach better when they have known times of failure. Many Christians will minister more when they have failed.

Much of the lack in Christian people is the lack of failure in their lives. Failure takes the hard parts of pride out of us. Not that Christians need to live in failure, but they need failure because they are human.

Jesus told Peter seated around the table at the Last Supper, Satan would have you, Peter, that he might sift you like wheat. But I have prayed for you that your faith fail not (Luke 22:32). Most of us spend time praying that we fail not, but Jesus spent His prayer praying that our *faith* fail not. Jesus showed no concern that Peter might fail, but that his faith might fail.

After the Resurrection, Jesus confronted Peter (John 21). If we take note, we are surprised by the conversation. It is not at all how most of us have been confronted or confront failure. Peter's denial of Jesus is not mentioned. No scolding, no rebuke for Peter's failure, but what is the concern on the heart of Jesus? "Simon, son of Jonas, loveth thou me?" (John 21:16). That is the question of importance. Has your faith failed you? Do you still love God after you have failed? The shipwreck was not the failure; to lose your love for God are the rocks upon which men destroy themselves. That is the loss that matters. The other failure, so what? It took out our arrogance, self-confidence, pride, and cockiness. Was that not good? May our faith not fail us.

STORAGE

After sifting, they took the wheat and placed it in storage jars set on a shelf or in a large harvest they buried the jars. There the wheat sat until needed for the next meal. The wheat was now pure and ready for use, but there it sat on the shelf or buried. Sound familiar? If it does not, you may never yet have made it to "bread."

Storage addresses the self-serving gratification of action. What you are is more important than what you do. Much Christian service has never gotten beyond what I can do for God. "What *am* I to God" is the question. In the end people are fed, not by things, but by bread. As long as you just do, you give things to people. When you become, you feed people.

Jesus once made bread for a great multitude of people (John 6:1–66). The multitude was fed, but they were not really fed, for soon they would be hungry again. Jesus then began to speak of who He was and how He was the true bread that feeds the world.

> "And Jesus said unto them, 'I am the bread of life: he that cometh to me shall never hunger; and he that believeth on me shall never thirst.'" (John 6:35)

This saying caused the Jews to murmur, because Jesus said He was the bread that came down from heaven. They couldn't see past the miracle their eyes had seen and the loaves they had eaten, which Jesus did not consider to be the miracle (John 6:26). To supply bread for people to eat for one day was a small thing to the real miracle of supplying bread for people to eat so they would never hunger again. The eating of what someone does for you can keep you from seeing the real miracle. Jesus said we were not to labor for the satisfaction which comes from doing, but to labor for the true satisfaction which the Son of man gives us (John 6:27). That satisfaction comes from what He makes us into, not just what natural blessings He does for us.

Jesus did such great things because of who He was. Men do great things trying to become great. Underlying both is an eternal truth. What a being is, is more important than what it does. Men seek to define what they are by what they do. Heaven defines what it does by what it is. The great gift offered to mankind by heaven is the power to become the sons of God (John 1:12).

There on the shelf these lessons are learned. The wheat sits there waiting. Waiting to be used. Learning that its value is in itself. Learning that it is loved because of what it is. Learning that meaning is in being, and that all that is done should come out of what we are.

The apostle Paul spoke of people who professed to know God but were to every good work reprobate (Titus 1:16). It was not that works were not being done, but that those works were reprobate because the people themselves were faulty. Ever since the fall of Adam, it has not been possible to restore the integrity of man by doing. To do quality works, a person first must be quality himself. Once a machine has failed and broken down, no amount of testing can ever ensure its absolute reliability. There will always be the chance that it will break down again. Running the machine, or doing, in our case, does not ensure wholeness, no matter how long you test the machine. Quality is something you are born or made with, coming first, before action, and so is more important. You need not be afraid you will be damaged on the shelf by the storage. When the pyramids were excavated in Egypt, stored grain was discovered. Some of this grain was planted and grew. It grew because it was quality, and the storing did not damage that.

Our concern is often with being used, while it should be with quality. A quality product always has a demand for it in this world. That is what is important. We spend our effort in the wrong area, when we should be expending it on becoming real.

Yet the shelf is not a place to plan on staying forever. Some make laws, either for themselves or in the churches, that shelf life is as far as things will go. On the shelf, things seem safe after all the wheat has been through up to this point. So some would settle in and make it an end in itself. It is here, while in storage in the jar, that the wheat all looks the same. Churches can be like that, too, in storage, looking the same, feeling the same, and in many other ways all similar. While in storage, the Church defines unity and oneness as sameness. This is really judging with outward judgment, with what the eyes see. Uniformity is not unity. Looking the same may make us feel better but does not really make for oneness. God intends a unity that touches the heart. To reach this unity requires the mill and the crushing of the shell of the wheat—all the more reason why some would wish to remain in the jar. But one day the divine hand with a divine appointment reaches for a jar of wheat and dumps some of it into the mill.

THE MILL

The mill is a rock grinding against another rock or hard place, crushing the wheat. Not as a friend does, one person against another, as in the proverb "*Iron sharpeneth iron; so a man sharpeneth the countenance of his friend*" (Prov. 27:17). No, the mill involves impersonal circumstances and situations crushing us from all sides. The mill is not a situation that would seem to be beneficial on the surface. It is not designed for the pleasure of the wheat but to make bread— that of many kernels being made one bread. True fellowship of the believer begins after the mill. This is brokenness, chastening that "*yieldeth the peaceable fruit of righteousness unto them which are exercised thereby*" (Heb. 12:11).

Here wheat is not crushed because it is bad, but on the very basis that it is good. Defective wheat is not crushed; only good wheat is crushed. Of what glory is it if we are buffeted for our faults and take it patiently? But when we do well and suffer for it, taking that suffering patiently, this is acceptable with God (1 Pet. 2:20). So also if the wheat has chaff on it, it is no glory to have it blown off, and if the wheat has stones in it, it is no glory to have them sifted out; but to be crushed because we are wheat is an honor.

This lesson must be learned while the wheat is buried: that value lies in the wheat itself. If we don't learn it while sitting on the shelf, we likely will bypass the mill for activity that gives a temporary sense of value. Such activity will thwart the bread making. A fundamental need of the human heart is to be loved not just for what it does, but for what it is. Persecution that brings honor to God comes from what we are and not primarily from what we do. Many have suffered righteously for their actions, but the full meaning and fulfillment of *"Rejoice ye in that day, and leap for joy: for, behold, your reward is great in heaven: for in the like manner did their fathers unto the prophets"* (Luke 6:23), comes to a believer with the realization that his persecution is not just for what he has done but for what he is as a believer. Perhaps it is the measure of pain involved that nips the bud of pride in the human heart and allows for such rejoicing at that moment of knowing how close we are to the heart of God. Often our wonder is stirred, that out of suffering those who believe can reach such a radiance and joy. How those who have been deeply broken can find such fountains of life is no mystery if we know the intimacies of their faith in God. Paradoxically, those who have not suffered in the will of God are really those who have missed out.

The Son of God laid down our example. He who was born in light, righteousness, and holiness still had need to learn obedience by the things he suffered (Heb. 5:8).

Christ began to speak of His death to His disciples, drawing from the Old Testament principle and applying it to Himself and to the New Testament Church. There was no chaff in His life that He must go to Jerusalem to have removed. Christ went to the cross to be broken because He was the perfect Lamb of God. Perfection itself was crushed that Bread could be made so the world might be fed. *"And I, if I be lifted up from the earth, will draw all men unto me"* (John 12:32).

Where Christ died was important. "For it cannot be," Jesus said, "that a prophet perish out of Jerusalem" (Luke 13:33). Christ went up to Jerusalem to die because that was the appointed place. It could not be otherwise. Jesus established the principle that not only is there a death but also a place for that death. It is in Jerusalem. We have no literal city where the temple is, but we have the temple. First Corinthians 3:16 says, *"Know ye not that ye are the temple of God, and that the Spirit of God dwelleth in you?"* The usage of the word *ye* is plural and not singular. You together are the temple of God. It is in the fellowship and gathering of the believers that a man finds Jerusalem and there finds a place where it is safe to die. The world supplies no such place; only the Church does.

We find another example of this pattern in the story of the Israelites crossing the Jordan River and preparing to attack the city of Jericho. It was there between the Jordan River and the city, well within reach of the warriors from Jericho, that God commanded Joshua to have all the children of Israel circumcised for the second time (Josh. 5:2–6). While the multitude was camped, and the enemy within range, every male was circumcised who had not come up out of Egypt with Moses. This act may well have put the male population out of feasible fighting condition for up to three days. During this time the surrounding enemy could have attacked and well might have prevailed. But the children of Israel were as safe in that camp as they ever were alone in the desert without any enemies. The reputation of Moses and Joshua had preceded the children of Israel, and circumcision was the last thing their enemies expected to be going on in the camp. There was safety in the camp.

It is the same when the Church walks in the fear of the LORD, under God. If the Church seeks approval and friendship with the world, it will never be a safe place for a man to be broken in. Safety comes from the unexpected angle; when the Church is effective it is feared, and the atmosphere is provided in which a man or woman can die with Christ.

It was the Spirit in Jesus Christ that caused Him to go up to Jerusalem, entering by a triumphal procession, eating the Last Supper with His disciples, afterward going to the garden, facing the law before both the religious and political leaders, suffering and enduring the shame of the cross. All these are steps that we follow as we follow the Master.

Death with Christ is a spiritual position obtained and entered into by faith. The apostle Paul said, "Knowing this, that our old man is crucified with him. . . ." (Rom. 6:6). It is useless to attempt death to the flesh outside of faith. The apostle said further, *"Likewise reckon ye also yourselves to be dead indeed unto sin. . . ."* (Rom. 6:11). But this reckoning is not done in the abstract but by faith unto a reality. So it cannot be that a man die alone in the desert, but in Jerusalem.

At the "mill," outside circumstances conspire to lock us in on all sides till there is no place for movement, that the outer shell might be crushed. People who always find their way out of trials and circumstances by wit and vigor will not be broken. It is those who walk in the law of the LORD who are crushed. It's a painful process—but would you not rather be bread?

A man once told God: "Look LORD, I wouldn't even spank my own son without telling him why." As he sat there that day he saw in his mind's eye a cross, and a man hanging on that cross saying, "My God, My God, why hast thou forsaken me?" And a voice spoke to his heart, "But I did."

The shell broke in that man's heart. All that hardness which makes us our own man shattered and fell. We would never dare walk this road if our Savior had not gone before us. But He has been here already; He has left the marks along the road that we can follow. If it is our foolishness that has brought us trouble, there is no thanks in that. But may God make us men who are *worthy* to suffer.

THE FLOUR

When the mill has done its grinding work, what you have left is not uniformity anymore, but true unity. You no longer have wheat but flour. What before was many kernels that looked alike and so felt as one now truly is one. It is possible for all to believe the same thing, go to the same church, and be brought up the same way, but only the mill makes us one with our brother. And that only if he also is broken.

> "Verily, verily, I say unto you, Except a corn of wheat fall into the ground and die, it abideth alone: but if it die, it bringeth forth much fruit." (John 12:24)

Then we can know what John meant when he said, "That ye also may have fellowship with us; and truly our fellowship is with the Father, and with his Son Jesus Christ" (1 John 1:3). It is the work of the mill that makes fellowship possible. Before that we were just canaries that sang the same tune, but canaries do not have fellowship.

After the mill has done its work, the flour is then sifted for the last time. This sifting is not to sift out the hard pieces, as it was for the wheat, but to sift the lumps out of the flour. These lumps are the cliques in a church, the unnatural joining together of only certain parts of the flour. When clicks form, freedom is lost. Flour must flow freely. So also broken people must flow freely together. Failure keeps the lumps out, lest we become exalted and lump together.

THE OIL

After the last sifting, oil is added to the flour. The oil is a representation of the Holy Spirit to be poured out upon the Body only when there is unity, not uniformity.

> "Behold, how good and how pleasant it is for brethren to dwell together in unity! It is like the precious ointment upon the head, that ran down upon the beard, even Aaron's beard: that went down to the skirts of his garments; As the dew of Hermon, and as the dew that descended upon the mountains of Zion: for there the LORD commanded the blessing, even life for evermore." (Ps. 133:1, 3)

Here in unity the oil is added to the wheat. It is also here that one of the greatest dangers happens to the process of bread making: the danger of adding yeast. We may have forgotten how to make bread without yeast, but God has not. It is the only kind of bread He uses.

The bread of ancient days was more like our crackers perhaps, flat and unleavened. People in those days knew how to make bread with yeast, but on the night Israel left Egypt, they were forbidden to put yeast in the bread made for the Passover supper.

Exodus 12:8: "*And they shall eat the flesh in that night, roast with fire, and unleavened bread; and with bitter herbs they shall eat it.*" After that Passover, Israel was commanded to observe the remembrance of the night of their deliverance with a feast of unleavened bread.

Exodus 12:17: "*And ye shall observe the feast of unleavened bread; for in this selfsame day have I brought your armies out of the land of Egypt: therefore shall ye observe this day in your generations by an ordinance for ever.*" This feast was to be observed for Israel's generations, but more than that it was an ordinance established forever. The people of God still observe this feast.

When God makes bread in the Church, He wants no yeast added. Yeast puffs up, making the dough full of air. Yeast is for appearances' sake, having no food value. Women put a little yeast in the dough and knead it in, which then goes throughout all of the dough. "*A little leaven leaveneth the whole lump*" (Gal. 5:9).

Much damage is done when the Church feeds the world leavened, puffed-up bread. Disillusionment sets in as people try the one food they expect to provide substance, but find instead only air.

The Yeast 5

What is wrong with placing yeast in the dough? How can all of God's work of purification be lost by yeast? After all, yeast has no quarrel with the flour and oil. It just wishes to add to what is already there.

> "Purge out the old leaven, that ye may be a new lump, as ye are unleavened. For even Christ our passover is sacrificed for us." (1 Cor. 5:7)

God deals in the "real," in that which has substance. The life of God is real. We are deceived by the yeast because puffed-up bread still contains bread and has the same ingredients—like puffed-up truth still is truth, just with something added to it. Sincere, well-intentioned people have thought error would be taken care of if they rejected all that opposed the truth, all the while not being aware that the greater deception is to defile the truth itself.

Perhaps the greatest defense against what is false is not the fear of being wrong, but the love of the truth itself. We have not yet learned to love truth if we add to it. Our minds and hearts are made with the capacity to love the truth. A heart un-wooed by that love is a heart unprotected.

Jesus said to beware the yeast of the Pharisees, Sadducees, and Herodians (Matt. 16:6; Mark 8:15). When the leaven comes in, the dough is defiled. It is tempting, when kneading the dough, to add some yeast, to take that which is real, ordinary, common, wholesome, and beloved and add to it. How the human heart is tempted by yeast.

The Beginning of the Yeast

This puffing up goes all the way back to the beginning, to the Garden of Eden, where God had made everything good and placed Adam and Eve in the midst of it. There the serpent asked Eve the question that undermined the stability of the world: "Yea, hath God said . . . ?" (Gen. 3:1). Other translations render it as, "Did God really say . . . ?" (NIV). The Living Bible says simply, "Really?"

It is a question that is cast as a slur against the sufficiency of the truth. Out of that slur came the defense Eve gave for the truth, revealing that she had already fallen for the implication within the question. She found it necessary to add to the truth.

Eve said, *"Ye shall not eat of it, neither shall ye touch it"* (Gen. 3:3). The touching part was not in the original commandment given by God. No doubt Eve thought to strengthen the truth by adding to it. The conversation went downhill from there and led to the defilement, by the choice of man, of the human race. We must be aware that defending truth may not be the best course of action. The truth is quite able to stand by itself. It is our part to stand with it. This is a much more humbling position but will save us in the end.

"We may eat of the fruit of the trees of the garden," Eve said, "But of the fruit of the tree which is in the midst of the garden, God hath said, Ye shall not eat of it" (Gen. 3:2–3). The commandment is so clear, so urgent, so definite, so defined, so limited in scope (just one tree), so hard to misunderstand, and yet so transgressed. What was it about the first of the human race that they could not just obey? Especially since obedience was first, and for the most part, not a negative, for the commandment was to eat of the fruit of every tree except one. What were the charms that so lured mankind away from the life lived in this garden? Though the lure is revealed in Scripture, we find with surprise that still today it draws upon the hearts of the descendants of those who fell.

The conversation continued between the serpent and Eve: "Ye shall not surely die," the serpent said. "For God doth know . . ." (Gen. 3:4, 5).

The serpent was saying, "God knows something that He's not telling you. There is information here that's missing and should be added. There is a world that can be expanded, which God is keeping from you. Why do you think God would be keeping it from you?"

The serpent continued and answered his own question: "That in the day ye eat thereof, then your eyes shall be opened, and ye shall be as gods, knowing good and evil" (Gen. 3:5).

Eve looked at the tree and saw that the lure itself was true. She could indeed add something to her life that was missing. There were three distinct ways in which this appeal of adding came to her. Eve saw that the tree was good for food, that it was pleasant to the eyes, and that it sparked a desire to make one wise. And she took of the fruit, ate, and gave also to her husband, and he ate (Gen. 3:6).

These three lures are the yeasts and are the same temptations Jesus faced in the desert. They are also the leaven of the Pharisees, the Sadducees, and the Herodians (Matt. 16:6; Mark 8:15). They are also the lusts of the world (1 John 2:16). Is not lust the desire to have what one does not have? More than that, it is the temptation to add to what one already has. This was the temptation Eve faced in the Garden of Eden.

We would do well to note that the devil took no stand against anything in the Garden. He criticized none of the fruit on the other trees. Nothing was said against the abundance God had given. The temptation was not to take away, but to add. Many in Christianity have missed this. We have thought of temptation primarily in terms of dropping the right to pick up the wrong, while the truth is that the beginning of sin comes usually as an addition to the right. The devil shows up in sheep's clothing, seemingly to carry on with God's work. He doesn't criticize what God has given to us as the Church. There is no mention made of leaving all the work up to this point—the threshing, the sifting, the mill—no problems with any of it. Just a little something to add that God has left out.

What is added will defile and pollute everything it touches. Disease, sickness, sin, murder, and all manner of wickedness came into the lives of mankind after the Garden of Eden, all from adding a little apple to their diet. Things have not changed.

YEAST IN THE GARDEN

Good for Food (Yeast #1)

The first thing the serpent showed Eve was that the forbidden fruit tasted good. Now Adam and Eve lacked nothing. Eve's taste buds were not somehow deprived. Hunger was not stalking her. This woman and man had a lot more and better things to eat than you and I.

So we must be honest at the beginning and admit that it is not because we are in such need that temptation pulls on us. That argument has already been tried and found faulty. It is not that we live in dire straits. God could give us everything we need as He did for Adam and Eve, to satisfy us completely, and yet temptation would draw on us, just like it drew on Eve in the middle of the Garden of Eden. Here the snake was able to convince Eve she was missing out. In the midst of the abundance of Eden, the likes of which you and I have never seen, this temptation came and it worked.

That is why a person can live in a growing church, sit under beneficial preaching, be ministered to, be well taught through Bible study, and still be drawn by the temptations of the world. Yeast draws not because we do not have, but because we have only what God has given.

The most basic honesty is often lacking in Christian circles along these lines. Much is made of the blessings of the LORD, and the implications made that he who is blessed of the LORD will find the offerings of the forbidden unattractive. Temptation appealed to Eve and it will appeal to us no matter how surrounded we are in blessings. If we as believers are not honest about the appeal of temptation, we set ourselves up for a fall. It is not that temptation is made to taste that much better than the right thing, but that it is made to look like something you would want to add to your life. All that tastes good may not be good for you. We should not be afraid to say so.

Pleasant to the Eyes (Yeast #2)

The second lure shown to Eve was that the fruit was pleasant to the eyes. We have a hard time following this because of how deprived we think we are. Our underlying assumption is that if God would just surround us with more pleasures, we would find sin unattractive. This was not true for Eve and it is not true for us. Eve lived in a beautiful place. Sunsets glowed such as we have never seen. Water, earth, trees, birds, and creatures of all forms were expressed in a way that we know little of. Beauty surrounded her. Yet in the midst of all this, the snake is able to convince her that she is missing out, that she is not seeing what she ought to see. Eve looked at the apple and saw a pleasant thing, and added it to her diet.

Seeing with your eyes the works of God will not keep you from the pull of temptation. Much is made in modern Christianity of showing people the works of God in order to convince them to follow God. This has a fallacy at its root, and keeps no one from temptation. We must look elsewhere for that. Believers often refrain from speaking the truth in its proper place, for fear someone will forsake God because things are hard for them. Because they want to show their love for someone, they try to surround them with blessings and good words. This is but again the theory that if our eyes could just see the plenty of God, we would not be tempted. That was already tried in the Garden of Eden and it did not work.

It is not that Christianity is poor or lacking of blessings. The heart of Christianity is rich; a richness, though, that is expressed with a sense of simplicity. This richness in Christianity is kept simple by the design of God Himself. The richness of the believer and his abundant supply are presented with the same naturalness and ordinariness that was in the Garden of Eden.

"O thou afflicted, tossed with tempest, and not comforted, behold, I will lay thy stones with fair colours, and lay thy foundations with sapphires. And I will make thy windows of agates, and thy gates of carbuncles, and all thy borders of pleasant stones." (Isa. 54:11–12)

The Church has always been given enough for her supply. The problem is that we are drawn away from that plenty because it is too ordinary, too everyday. So the yeast has its drawing. But like those who have bitten into a loaf full of air, so is the promise of yeast, and as unfulfilling.

"Comfort ye, comfort ye my people, saith your God. Speak ye comfortable to Jerusalem, and cry unto her, that her warfare is accomplished, that her iniquity is pardoned: for she hath received of the LORD's hand double for all her sins." (Isa. 40:1–2)

It's no use speaking of making things easier for people, which much of Christianity does. The yeast of the serpent will still have an attraction. It is the heart that must be drawn again by the love of the truth and recaptured by God. Until then the hiss of the serpent that something is missing will cause us to stop and listen.

To make one wise (Yeast #3)

The third lure shown to Eve was that the fruit of the tree was to be desired to make one wise. Again, it was not the lack of wisdom drawing her but the lust to appear wiser than she was. In the Garden, Eve walked with God in a literal way. In the cool of the day, the Almighty Himself walked with Adam and Eve. They enjoyed an intimate relationship. Adam had named all the animals, and God had called it good. None of us has ever done that. Yet, here the snake was able to convince Eve that she needed something more—something to make her wiser still—to feel like somebody. "Your self-esteem," the serpent might say in our day, "will go up. Just eat the fruit."

Great and mighty revelation is no protection against this transgression. The apostle Paul himself had to be given a thorn in the flesh, lest he become puffed up. Great usage by God, education, degree, knowledge, long face, pious dress, deep understanding—nothing removes this temptation from us. It is an easy observable fact that the portions of Christianity most openly into dreams, revelations, angels, and so-called Spirit, are perhaps the most deceived. Spiritual knowledge of God did not keep Eve from temptation, and it will not keep you and me from it. It is arrogance indeed to think otherwise.

The problem is the real that we have around us and fail to appreciate—the mercy we walk in, the graces bestowed upon our life. God comes that way. He goes with us and looks so ordinary, so part of our life. The blessings of God are where we live and work. It is sin that is out of the ordinary. Sin puts the twang in, the peculiar flavor that good does not. The lie is the yeast.

Jesus gave us further understanding of these three yeasts when He warned his disciples about the leaven of the Pharisees, the Sadducees, and of Herod (Matt. 16:11; Mark 8:15). When Jesus bade his disciples to beware, they understood Him to mean natural bread. It was not about natural bread that He spoke, but about the doctrine of the Pharisees, the Sadducees, and of Herod.

THE THREE DOCTRINES

The Doctrine of Herod

The offer in the Garden to taste the fruit, we find in Herod in quite full-blown form. Though the indulgences of Herod are taken to an extreme, perhaps, it is to our peril to assume that the tastes of the flesh pose no temptations for the dedicated believer. With shocking regularity, the most basic transgressions turn up in professing Christian circles. Not just beginners are falling, which one might expect, but also the well-established and successful believers, showing us again that plenty is no security against temptation.

Herod was a king in a series of four kings noted for their debaucheries and fleshly lusts. One of them had ten wives. One of them murdered his immediate family. The children of Bethlehem were killed by Herod. The cruelest member of these kings was Herod Agrippa I, whose death is told of in Acts 12:20–23. The angel of the LORD smote him, and he was eaten by worms.

Fornications, uncleanness, inordinate affections, evil concupiscence, covetousness, pornography, drugs, immorality, and cruelty are not unknown among the most pious of the religious world. Cruelty should not be passed over too quickly, either. Though we are told to love mercy (Mic. 6:8), believers are quite capable of cruelty, because it tastes good. These sins are quite alive and well in circles where, from the natural mind's perspective, you would least expect to find them.

Many a believer, who thought he was quite close to the finish line, having grown past any danger of these basic sins, has yet fallen—for they taste good. For here at the end, when the dough is almost ready for baking in the fire, yeast threatens. We may have walked in faith for many years, yet when we think temptation should be gone it is not. "Wherefore let him that thinketh he standeth take heed lest he fall" (1 Cor. 10:12). Even after success in the kingdom of God, we still feel the pull of temptation that offers what we might be missing. "The world is passing you by," it says. With such thoughts the appetite is whetted to partake of something that promises to add to our satisfaction.

Church benches are no cure for this leaven. It doesn't take a lot, just a little, and it gets in and defiles the whole thing. "A little leaven leaveneth the whole lump" (Gal. 5:9).

The Doctrine of the Sadducees

The temptation in the Garden to see what is pleasing to the eyes—above what God has given—is found in the doctrine of the Sadducees. Our eyes see of possessions, money, treasure, lands, and all things material. God has given us material things, but whether rich or poor, the temptation is in the promise of security and growth in possessions, not in the mere possessions themselves. Apparently no one can quite succeed in bringing this temptation in its base form into the believer's life, as is the case with the doctrine of Herod, so it must be made a religious thing, as the doctrine of Herod usually is not.

The Sadducees were therefore religious, although not in the sense that we might think. Their religion consisted of confidence placed in the power of things. Religious emotion and faith in the supernatural were left out. They had no belief or faith in the oral Law, as did the Pharisees, acknowledging only the first five books of Genesis. They had no belief in angels, spirit beings, or even resurrection. The apostle Paul used them in his trial before the council to create a division between his persecutors on the issue of the resurrection.

> "And when he had so said, there arose a dissension between the Pharisees and the Sadducees: and the multitude was divided." (Acts 23:7)

The Sadducees had turned the love of money and things into a religion, or in our words, made them acceptable in the life of a believer. You could now love the things known to be wrong if seen in the world, but since they were made spiritual it was OK. The marriage of the Pharisee and the Sadducee is similar to the marriage of the businessman and the preacher of modern Christianity. Some preachers would despise touching the money of the world, but make it "Christian" money, and it's OK. A strict separation is kept between the preacher and his supporting businessmen, just as between the Pharisees and the Sadducees. The businessman is not to preach, and the preacher is not to work for money, but together they are in agreement.

The responsibility for the care of the temple money and temple selling and buying was the Sadducees'. When Jesus drove out of the temple those who sold and bought, He was driving out Sadducees. Some believe that this incident sparked the union between the Sadducees and Pharisees to finally bring about the capture of Jesus. It is still so today—when the true gospel hurts both the religious and the money, the two come together to hinder the truth.

The apostle Paul spoke of men who were of corrupt minds and destitute of the truth, supposing that gain is godliness (1 Tim. 6:5). The love of money is the love of gain. Money gives you what you can see. So men place great confidence in money, because it buys gain and progress. Much of the growth in Christianity comes in non-visible ways, in ways that the eyes may not perceive at the moment. Yet the years will reveal great growth that will shine in comparison to the momentary gain purchased with money.

"But what things were gain to me," said Paul, "Those I counted loss for Christ" (Phil. 3:7). The apostle is referring not just to things purchased with money, but to things purchased by inheritance, by stock, by circumcision, by law, and by zeal. These are of the yeast of the Sadducees, which the eye lusts to look upon. The security of the believer is by faith in Christ, yet the temptation pulls upon us to add a security we can see, purchased with money, circumcision, law, zeal, or by inheritance.

People rich in natural talent, money, abilities, and such are often given high position in the church—because they are rich, not because they are spiritual. The abundance of the supply of the natural is no sure evidence of the blessing of God. Money should not talk in church. The spiritual man should talk. But if we think we can throw out the rich people and so silence the talk of money, we are fooling ourselves. Our hearts may still be lusting after the money.

The Sadducees didn't believe in many things sacred to a Pharisee, but they were tolerated because they had things to give. They kept the temple in money and paid the bills, and that gave otherwise non-religious people a reason to come to church. Someone who had no belief in angels, the oral Law of that time, and the resurrection of the dead would have been thrown out without question, but not if he was rich. The Pharisees tolerated the Sadducees, even though it looked like an obvious contradiction, and the Sadducees tolerated the Pharisees, even though they normally would have no time for such people. Why did they do it? Because each benefited the other, and so it still is today. In the same church can be both, the rich and the religious.

The Scripture says there is a thinking that supposes gain to be godliness. From such we are instructed to withdraw ourselves (1 Tim. 6:5). That is not to imply that all gain is ungodly, but today's mentality is to produce things quickly, to prosper right away, to develop a gift in record time to have something to show someone. Producing things that can be seen, to demonstrate one's level of spirituality—that is yeast. When this bread is tasted it will be found to have air throughout.

The Doctrine of the Pharisees

The temptation in the Garden to be wiser than the wisdom given us by God we find as the doctrine of the Pharisees. It is not that God is against wisdom; we are told to ask of God, who gives liberally, for wisdom if we lack it (James 1:5). It is not the lack of supply that causes temptation. It is our dissatisfaction with what God has supplied. So man is drawn into the temptation to acquire wisdom in addition to the supply of God. It must be noted that such people always have much that is right in regards to God's wisdom; it is the addition that contains the yeast and defiles all of the bread.

The Pharisees had their law and appeared to be wise spiritually, with a wisdom of those who are old in spiritual growth. Not only did they obey the written Law, they added more on top. What was added was revealed to be the most important to them when Jesus rebuked them for obeying the added over the written. As Jesus told them, "Thus have ye made the commandment of God of none effect by your tradition" (Matt. 15:6). This was the yeast that had gone throughout the bread and become more important than the bread itself.

The Pharisees made their robes longer than other people, loved to be greeted in the streets, got the best seats at the meeting house and rooms at the feasts (Luke 20:46). They said prayers on street corners (Matt. 6:5). They fasted openly with a sad countenance, disfiguring their faces, and not washing so people would know they were fasting (Matt. 6:16). They went down to give alms with trumpets blowing before them so people would know what they were doing (Matt. 6:2).

These were men about whom Jesus said quite weighty things that we might not find fitting. Things such as: You bind heavy burdens and grievous to be borne on men's shoulders, but you yourselves will not move them with one of your fingers (Matt. 23:4). You shut up the kingdom of heaven for others, yet will not go in yourselves, but try to stop those who are entering from going in (Matt. 23:13). You devour widows' houses, and to cover up make long prayers (Matt. 23:14). You travel over land and sea to make a convert, and when you make one you make him twice the child of hell you yourselves are (Matt. 23:15). You are hypocrites, for you make the outside of the cup clean, but inside the cup is full of plunder and want of self control. You look righteous outside where men can see you, but on the inside you really are full of hypocrisy and evil (Matt. 23:25, 27). You are serpents, and a generation of vipers, and cannot escape the damnation of hell (Matt. 23:33).

What was it about the Pharisees that invoked such words from Jesus? Would we have thought they deserved such treatment if we had lived in those days? Would we today think Pharisees actually that bad? This is the last of the three yeasts. Is it because this is the most deceptive, and therefore, the most dangerous yeast that Jesus spent the most time on it and had the strongest words to say about it? Must it perhaps lie closest to our own hearts and admirations?

The story is told of a Jew who survived Hitler's Holocaust and went up to look at Adolf Eichmann at his trial. Eichmann had been the manager of "The Final Solution" for the extermination of Jews. After seeing Eichmann, the Jew came away greatly shaken. His friends asked him, "Did Eichmann look so terrible, that you are so shaken?" "No," said the man. "He looked just like me."

In serving God, where the best intentions of man lie, there the greatest danger is found. For to all those who sincerely desire to follow the laws of God belongs the danger of the doctrine of the Pharisees. It is a yeast most insidious. To grow old with God, you must walk with Him, and the process cannot be pushed along faster by adjusting the outside to look like inward progress. Once you place your confidence in the outward to measure your success, the thing will snowball out of control. The outside gives less confidence than the inside, and the more confidence placed on the outside the less confidence it gives, so the more confidence you must place on it. As the satisfaction decreases the activity must increase, until someone dares speak the truth about the air in your life, and then you will thumb your nose at him and say, "I am a holy man."

Is being on time for worship more important than stopping to help a man beaten up by robbers (Luke 10:30–36)? Are you among those who with religious fervor condemn a woman caught in adultery with stoning (John 8:3)? No one knows for sure, but might it have been the sins of those men who brought the woman that Jesus was writing on the dirt (John 8:6)?

The Pharisees still have as great a following as they ever had. Not followers of their deeds necessarily, but admirers who pay deference to their accomplishments. From the politicians, to the church people, to the man on the street, there is great admiration, not for obeying the commandments of God, but for what is added on the outside. The admiration for an outward display of piety is as prevalent today as ever; the lust to be wiser than God has made you to be and appear as something you are not.

If you begin the setting of times, ways, and structures as a measure of spiritual growth, you will feel the approval of the world rise around you. They may not follow you in the same practice, but their applause will give you legitimacy. As a general rule, the more austere you make your outward life, the more you will be admired by those around you.

Except we become as little children and trust in the Father's supply and care for us, let us not think that we shall enter the kingdom of God (Mark 10:15). When the Bible speaks of the kingdom of God, it is not speaking just of the life to come after this earthly life, but of the life lived with God while on this earth. Here and now we do not really begin to walk with God until our hearts become as children's hearts. The heart of a Pharisee is not the heart of a child. The heart of a Pharisee is a heart wise and all grown up without God.

THE WILDERNESS VICTORIES

When we go to the fourth chapter of Luke we find the temptations of Christ that were brought to Him by the devil. The setting is now the New Testament, and the temptations are directed towards the second Adam, not the first. God is not going back to the Garden to engage the devil there. In restoring man, the battle now will be fought in the desert. Creation has fallen, and in redeeming mankind God will not repeat Himself. The temptations of Christ are the same temptations of the Garden, and yet different, because the order is different. The level of the temptation has been greatly raised and is no longer just simply a transgression of the Law in eating an apple. Satan, in speaking to Christ, speaks to the Word incarnate itself (1 Tim. 3:16). It is of no use for the devil to speak to Christ of fornications, adulteries, murders, lying, and deceit. For the first Adam was made a living soul, but the last Adam was made a quickening Spirit (1 Cor. 15:45). So we are shown in Christ the full extent of the temptation of yeast.

In the Garden we see the beginnings of the temptations of yeasts. In the doctrines of Herod, Sadducees, and Pharisees, we see the degree to which man has succumbed to those temptations. And in the temptations of Christ, we see Christ drawing the devil out fully and defeating him at the highest level of those temptations.

"And Jesus being full of the Holy Ghost returned from Jordan and was led by the Spirit into the wilderness, Being forty days tempted of the devil. And in those days he did eat nothing: and when they were ended, he afterward hungered." (Luke 4:1–2)

The First Temptation

"And the devil said unto Him, If thou be the Son of God, command this stone that it be made bread. And Jesus answered him saying, 'It is written that man shall not live by bread alone but by every word of God.'" (Luke 4:3–4)

Christ is not being tempted to eat a forbidden apple because it was good for food. This temptation of Christ concerns bread, and bread is not forbidden to eat as the apple was forbidden to eat. God and men had been making bread throughout the Old Testament. God had supplied manna in the desert. David had eaten the showbread when he was hungry. Unleavened bread would be eaten at the first Passover, and Christ Himself would break bread at the last supper He ate with His disciples. There is no law against eating bread. The transgression is not there.

As the temptation is drawn out, we see what it really is—a transgression not just of a commandment of God, but a transgression of the way God does things. It is an attack, not just on what God does, but on how He does it. God has made bread, but He has never made bread out of stone. He never did and never will, and neither did Jesus. God makes bread out of wheat, and Jesus was not going to violate that order. In the same way, Jesus would never heal anybody except the way God had done so in the first place. No cripple would walk, no blind person would see, no leper be cleansed, and no devil cast out except through Christ doing what He had seen the Father do (John 5:19). That day on the hillside when in His hands the loaves and fishes were multiplied, wasn't He doing what the Father does daily—multiplying from the seed of wheat and the seed of fish, making many out of few? Jesus was doing it God's way, not from rocks, as the devil would have Him do.

This does matter. We have lost something in the Church if we do not teach the full extent of the will of God. Obedience has been made into some sterile action, a passive stance that has left many numb. Jesus came, as it is written in the volume of the book, "To do the will of God" (Heb. 10:7). It does matter not just what we do, but how we do it.

The place of the temptation of the believer is not the Garden but the desert. It makes no difference how hungry you get in the desert, nor how dry and dusty it is. You cannot give in to the temptation of getting bread outside of the way or will of God. Our minds struggle with this, but it cannot be passed over. Many Christians, in the desert of their lives, would not think of fornication, adultery, or drunkenness, yet still they sell out for bread made from stones, because they are hungry and think it makes no difference how they came by the bread as long as it is bread. The heart of the sin of the lusts of the flesh is really violating the ways of God, and they start long before you ever pick up the dirty magazine or get in bed with someone other than your wife. If the Church would but look, it would find that it has left the ways of God before the other shows up. There is something going on, Jesus is teaching us in this temptation, which is greater than my hunger. It is the way of God. And if I cannot come by bread made the right way, then I go hungry. It does matter how God does things, and the desert is the test.

The devil said it does not matter—you're in a desert and you're hungry. God does not forbid the eating of bread. So, if you really are the Son of God, here is a stone, make it into bread. But Jesus said, "It is written man shall not live by bread alone but by every word of God" (Luke 4:4). There is a cause greater than even my life. It does matter.

If we fail the test, we open the door in the Church to the flesh. We should not be surprised at this, as this transgression is of the same spirit that produces the indulgences of Herod. Only now, because the transgression has been made on a higher level, the results may be first of a higher caliber. Let us not think the old-fashioned sins are very far behind.

It does matter not just that we are Christians, but how we are Christians. People are being deceived by the droves, because they are hungry in the desert for bread, and it matters no longer to them how they get bread, as long as they get it. Bread made from stones is bread made with yeast in it—empty, puffed up, and unsatisfying bread.

God knows the lack of bread, perhaps, where you and I may be living today. But according to the Scripture, Christ was led, and it is possible for us to be led, into the desert by the Spirit of God to be tested. When in the desert are we going to put our own desires first? What is the passion of our lives? Just to fill our stomachs, physical or otherwise? Or is there something greater going on? Is our heart hungry for the ways of God? It is now a desert and not a garden that tests that question.

Is there anything in you that would learn of God and His ways? Is it important enough for you to take the time to do it? If what you want is not in the ways of God, will you follow your appetite? Will the hunger of the desert drive you into the arms of false prophets and false teachers, as long as they produce something for you to eat? Will the hunger for bread cause you to turn to the stones, the hurts and hard times in your life for nourishment? Our hope is in God and not in sufferings. Although God uses trials, it is strange bread that is made out of such stones. Our comfort comes from heaven, not in false prophets, or in how much we have suffered.

Jesus is not about to make bread out of stone. You may think it a small thing, but God does not. No longer is surface obedience to a commandment in the Garden enough. We are not there anymore. Now we must know God. Jesus said, "And this is life eternal, that they might know thee the only true God, and Jesus Christ, whom thou hast sent" (John 17:3).

The Second Temptation

"And the devil, taking him up into an high mountain, showed unto him all the kingdoms of the world in a moment of time. And the devil said unto him, All this power will I give thee, and the glory of them: for that is delivered unto me: and to whomsoever I will I give it. If thou therefore wilt worship me, all shall be thine. And Jesus answered and said unto Him, Get thee behind me Satan for it is written thou shalt worship the LORD thy God and Him only shalt thou serve." (Luke 4:5–7)

In this, the second temptation the devil brought to Jesus, the offer is for things outside of the time of God. The temptation has been drawn out to its full extent to show us what is really at the root of this yeast: the worship of things. That is why Jesus said we cannot love God and money at the same time, because both are worship, and we cannot serve two things at the same time (Matt. 6:24).

Again, there is no forbidden apple in this temptation that sparks desire. Jesus knew that all things were to be His by the Father (Matt. 11:27). The time would come when the Father would give to Jesus all power and all glory and all might, both in heaven and in the earth (Eph. 1:20–22). These things offered to Christ by the devil, and much, much more, were His right, but they were subject to the timing of God. The things offered by the devil were not forbidden, but their *worship* was forbidden, and the question of whether we worship them is answered in whether we can *wait* until God provides in His own time. We are told to "seek . . . first the kingdom of God and his righteousness" (Matt. 6:33), and the meaning is to wait on the rest that shall be added to us. The violation is not the things offered, as some Christians, who reject the holding of certain possessions, still think. That is a Garden-of-Eden mentality. In the meantime, those who believe that way and reject some possessions, may well have all kinds of worship in their hearts for the things that they do have (or do not have), be they small or great. Satan knew that worship was the heart of the matter. He knew, too, that Jesus would one day be Lord of all things, but meanwhile he offered what he no doubt thought Jesus craved, as he himself did. "Worship me," the devil said, "All shall be thine" (Luke 4:7). The heart of the matter was worship, and Christ would not worship anything other than God, even to obtain what was His right to have. Can we say the same? Our waiting answers the question.

Are we willing to wait until God gives it? We are in need, we are in the desert, the years and the days are going by. Will we maneuver, jockey, and manipulate events to get things? To get a certain outcome in church matters or otherwise? What about the money we need? Much of the praying and fasting of Christians is no different from the oriental herbs, crystals, ying and yang, water witching, biomagnetics, and many other such things that the heathen do (and, sadly, now many even in the Church do). It is of the same spirit— the bending of the knee to get what I want. The devil is behind it all, receiving the worship. For when we worship to get things, Christ has shown us, it is worship of the devil.

Worship is to reverence and give honor. There are people to whom this is due, such as parents (Luke 18:20), elders (1 Tim. 5:3, 17), and kings (1 Pet. 2:17). The temptation of the yeast concerns giving reverence and honor to people for the express purpose of getting something from them, whether favors, good reports, positions, money, or anything else. That is what is wrong. Jesus said, "How can ye believe, which receive honor one of another, and seek not the honor that cometh from God only?" (John 5:44). The sinful honor-seeking that Jesus spoke of was not the honor one gives to parents, rulers, or leaders for their own sakes, but the honor one gives and receives for the purpose of receiving things. Much of Christianity has lost its fear of the danger of worship in order to receive things by a clever twist someone has placed on the subject. Christian literature and philosophy is, by and large, occupied with what writers perceive as the danger of the ownership of things. This is not the temptation. Our thoughts and concerns are directed to the ownership of things—whether I have too many, or whether my neighbor has too many—when all the time the real yeast is being brought right by our noses as we daily give honor and worship to men for the receiving of many things, whether we actually own many possessions or not. The real temptation is not the ownership of things, but the worship given to receive things. Even the heathen kneeling in front of his idol would not stay there a minute if he thought it was only a block of wood and he was not going to get something. So we would not do many of the things we do, if we did not think we were getting something out of it. The heathen is worshiping to receive things, whether rain or revenge on his enemies. How much of our meetings, praying, and reverence that we give to men is done to receive blessings, whether acceptance in a group or assurance of spiritual growth. We would not stay on our knees, either, if we thought we would get nothing.

Christians often get tired of the desert with its constant heat and dryness, and with having so little to show for the Christian life that the world counts as valuable. The desire of man is for something to show the world, to silence the talking, to hush the voices of how nothing is being done. Waiting on God is not the same as sitting around allowing one's Christian life to run downhill, but the devil will call it the same. Many believers in the Church are not longing to please God, but are lusting for positions, ministries, callings, gifts, anointings, and other such things, without ever seeing the worship they are giving for those things, and the devil is behind it all. Jesus said, "Thou shalt worship the LORD thy God only." That means waiting on God to meet my need whatever the conditions and whatever His time.

Scripture warns greatly against going to places where God is not, but where it is reported He is. "For there shall arise false Christs, and false prophets, and shall show great signs and wonders; inso much that if it were possible, they shall deceive the very elect. Behold I have told you before. Wherefore if they shall say unto you, Behold, he is in the desert; go not forth: behold, he is in the secret chambers; believe it not" (Matt. 24:24–26).

It is very accepted in our time to run to and fro all over the place, sampling everything that is going on in the church world, in search of gifts and callings. What is driving all this is a great hunger for things, be they physical manifestations or spiritual; the desire is to have. That attitude of worship is given to places where God is said to be moving, and to people through whom it is said that God is moving, all in pursuit of a calling or spiritual blessing. Really, we should not be surprised then when it is all over, and we see under the bottom of it all that money is the root, for it all springs from the Garden of Eden and from the lust of the Sadducees. We should know that when God calls, He offers Himself, not things; those things may be in Him, but they are released in His time, not by our desire.

The will of God involves the timing of God. If we cannot stand the timing of God, then we cannot stand the will of God.

The Third Temptation

> "And he brought Him to Jerusalem and sat Him on the pinnacle of the temple and said unto Him, If thou be the Son of God, cast thyself down from thence for it is written, He shall give His angels charge over thee to keep thee, and in their hands they shall bear thee up lest at any time thou shalt dash thy foot against a stone. And Jesus answered and said unto Him, It is said, thou shalt not tempt the Lord thy God." (Luke 4:9–12)

The temptation in the Garden to eat an apple to make one wise has now moved well beyond that. Jesus has drawn out fully the devil and his temptation. No longer is it an apple that the devil wants man to use, but the promises and the word of God itself, to look wise. The question is, are we willing to use the grace and miracles that God has given us to make ourselves look good? If we are willing to use the things of God to look good on the outside, then we will lose out on the inside, where dwells true spirituality. That is why Jesus called the Pharisees hypocrites. They were using the written word, and what they claimed was the written word, to produce a righteousness before men. "Even so ye also outwardly appear righteous unto men, but within ye are full of hypocrisy and iniquity" (Matt. 23:28). Man is selfish and willing to use the most sacred things of God to imitate the character of God and appear to be righteous. That is why Jesus used such strong language about the Pharisees (Matt. 23:33). The seemingly harmless eating of an apple in the Garden has been shown to be what it really is—an affront against the person of God. That man could think in his mind that he can imitate the righteousness of God is a marvel indeed, but that is what the devil would propose for us to do and join him in his opinion that the nature of God is really just an imitation, too. God is not an imitation, but is real, and we will be made into His image by the grace of His hand and not by our own hand.

The devil told Jesus to jump from the pinnacle of the temple by His own choosing. Jesus was not opposed to relying on and trusting in God. In fact, He trusted God to a much greater extent than jumping off the temple. But He was not about to use His relationship with God to show off and look good to men. Such a thing tempts God and tries Him. The temple is where the children of Israel came to worship. Would it not have looked grand if Jesus had jumped off the top of the temple and landed safely in the middle of the worshipers? People would have, and still do, follow a man gladly who can do such demonstrations of his power.

The devil is telling Jesus, if You go to the pinnacle and jump off landing safely, everybody will see Your glory right away, and You will accomplish Your mission on the earth quickly. You are the Son of God, aren't You? Use His power to establish Yourself.

Jesus would not violate the person of God by using the promises of God to better His own position in the eyes of men. "You shall not tempt the LORD your God," He said. "You shall not use His things for your own purposes, to look wise."

Christians use prayers, fasting, alms, clothing, methods, training, promises, traditions, tithing, obedience, faith, love, and anything pertaining to righteousness as a copy and an imitation to make themselves look wise and advanced in the ways of God, and so provoke the patience and wrath of God. Religious clothes ought never impress the Church as righteousness as it impresses the world.

The desert may be dry, dusty, and forsaken, with temptation all around. That is never a justification to start jumping off temples so other people will think we are more spiritual than we are. We must be honest about where we are in spiritual growth. Jesus said the seed of God would grow and bear fruit in the good ground, and the good ground was an honest and good heart (Luke 8:15). The processes of God are not a quick thing to be completed in a moment of time. Fakeness sells in the world, but it ought to have no part in the Church. It is wrong to use the Word of God and the promises of God to imitate the character of God, to pretend to be something we are not.

The Yeast

LOVE NOT THE WORLD

"Love not the world, neither the things that are in the world. If any man love the world, the love of the Father is not in him for all that is in the world, the lust of the flesh, and the lust of the eyes, and the pride of life, is not of the Father but is of the world. And the world passes away and the lust thereof. But he that doeth the will of God abideth forever." (1 John 2:15–17)

The apostle John sums up all three temptations in this Scripture. All are lusts, all are of the world, and all are not of the Father. We are told to love neither the world nor the things in it. The world is the lust to indulge oneself outside of the ways of God, the lust for things outside of the time of God, and the lust for righteousness outside of the person of God.

Lust comes in an instant but is gone before long and does not endure, leaving only bondage. Living, the opposite of lust, brings with it freedom and liberty. Often we are as was said of a man, "With scarce a notion of what liberty really is. He did not know that it was to be found in law—neither social, natural, nor moral law, but the law of liberty—oneness with the will and design which are our existence—these no arbitrary appointment, no invention of even the one who has the power to make, but the reproduction in increased degree of the same glorious necessities of existence as his own—the making of him in the very image of his maker. For the truth of God is the life of man" (*Donal Grant*, George MacDonald, Sunrise Books, 1990).

How few of us learn what living is. We consume most of our life pursuing lust. What is living? To find and walk in the ways of God. To rest in the time of God. To know God. These are life eternal. Heaven would impart to us its liberty, but here again our concept of liberty may be skewed. What the world calls liberty is not liberty: sin has never set anyone free. Nor is liberty what religion tells us: learning to like whatever flavor of restraint it offers. Liberty is found in law, in the law of existence. Not some law made up by society, or a law of nature, or a law that a certain religion has decreed; nor is it even a law made up by God Himself, who has power to create anything. Even God did not make this law, the law of liberty—rather, He gives it away in ever increasing degrees to anyone who will receive it. It is the power to be, or as the apostle John says so well, "But as many as received him, to them gave he power to become the sons of God, even to them that believe on his name" (John 1:12). This is the highest law, the law of existence. In the Old Testament there was no higher name for God than the one given to Moses at the burning bush: "And God said unto Moses, I AM THAT I AM" (Exod. 3:14). This is the process of God, to make us into the very image of Him who is what He is. God did not create His own existence, nor did anyone else, so His life can never be taken away. The life of God is therefore an absolute law, and also absolutely free. There is, then, no higher law than liberty, for there is no higher life than God, from which it comes. To be free is to live, and to live is to be free.

Why do we understand this so little in the Church? Often we act as if we were trying to manufacture the children of God, both in others and in ourselves. Have we never watched birds fly? They do it with such grace and beauty, for as we know, they enjoy great freedom to fly. What then of the airplane that soars by? No one thinks of its freedom, because an airplane will never be free—for it will never live. The one was born in a nest, and the other was made in a hanger. One is alive and free, and the other is dead and earth bound, though both fly through the air. What kind of Christians are we becoming? Free and living or dead and mechanical? Will we listen to the world that promises us freedom but offers only dead lusts, or will we listen to God who offers us eternal and unchangeable laws that, like the wings of a bird, lift us into the wind of life? God can grow these laws in us that we might be like He is, free and living.

After the Oil

After the oil has been added and the yeast kept out, the bread is at the dough stage. You can put your fingers on the dough and it leaves marks. So it is with believers before they have been through fire. Dough is not meant to be the finished product, as dough absorbs the surrounding influences. As fire and heat are needed for the dough, so also they are needed for the believer that the outside world cannot come and push and leave its mark. For the dough to be finished it is taken, placed in a pan, and put in an oven. Fire is needed so the finished product is breakable bread and not concrete. Concrete sets up in any normal day, so many believers just get hard and set in day-to-day humdrum living. But the fire produces high-quality bread—as well as believers. The fire places pressure and heat on the dough from all sides, and not just from any given point. That is the experience of fire in contrast to other trials up to this point. It is hard to identify the direction of the heat of the oven, as it comes from all over and is continuous and constant.

"Beloved, think it not strange concerning the fiery trial which is to try you, as though some strange thing happened unto you. . . ." (1 Pet. 4:12)

The fiery trial involves more a period of our lives than a particular event happening apart from the whole. So it is perhaps more difficult to deal with than just a single trial. In a single trial it is often much easier to find God and feel His presence than in the fire. In the fiery trial the most common tormented cry is "Where is God?" Before this it seemed like God was always there somewhere and we could talk to Him. When we are going through the mill, the winnowing, and the threshing, we can always seem to find Him and talk to Him. God could talk with us. But in the fire it seems like God is not there. It is a very difficult thing. We can pray and seek God, but where is the contact?

We are like the dough in the pan. The pan holds the dough through the fire, and after the loaf of bread comes out of the oven and is shaken off the pan, it has the print of the pan on it and is not susceptible to other prints as before. So it is with us. The reason we have trouble finding God in the fire is because we are in His hands and are looking too far out for God. God is there in the fire with us, and when we come out of the fire the prints of His hands will be on us. We will no longer, for that area and time, take on the prints of others.

When Jesus was tried in the fire, the experience was not known as a single episode, but the story is told of an entire week—that of Jesus entering Jerusalem riding on a donkey to the supper He had with His disciples, the garden, the capture, the trial, the betrayal, the crucifixion, His death, and His burial. Toward the end Jesus gave that heart-rending cry already recorded in the Old Testament but now lived out in the life of the Son of God: "My God, my God, why hast thou forsaken me" (Ps. 22:1; Mark 15:34). It was not, as has been said, that Jesus was God-forsaken, but it was that He had to feel God-forsaken. Jesus died in faith when He said, "Father into thy hands I commend my spirit" (Luke 23:46). Just as we in the fire must rest in faith, sight will do us no good. It is a strange thing indeed, but none the less true that the closer we are to God the more we walk by faith. The old saints and those rich in God have told us that the end gets dim around the eyes, but brighter around the heart. So the fire was to Jesus the final makings of bread in Himself. As He said, "And I, if I be lifted up from the earth, will draw all men unto me" (John 12:32). For us also as believers, small areas and periods of our lives can be made ready by the fire for ministry to others. We can then be broken to feed the world. We must be careful of boasting of things that do not really happen to us, as it is doubtful any of us ever are completely sanctified as Jesus was, but we are called to be partakers in even a small way of the heavenly calling. We too can be bread to our world.

After the fire we have the mark of God on us and are no longer "children tossed to and fro and carried about with every wind of doctrine" (Eph. 4:14). We are now ready to be broken to feed the world.

Believers sit in pews of churches and enter Christianity thinking how wonderful it must be and how glorious to serve God. This is all true, but what is normally on their minds are the supposed chills and thrills that surely must go up and down one's spine in God's service—and how the flesh will glory when it is become a saint. But to be a saint is to be broken and used to feed the world with bread. That isn't glorious to the flesh, but is glorious because it is the will of God. We will by now have the will of God as our strength, as Jesus did when He said, "I have meat to eat that ye know not of" (John 4:32). Otherwise we would not have progressed this far.

We have been given grace and mercy and the seed of the Word of God that we might have a harvest, and out of that harvest to make bread in our generation, that our children might live and make bread themselves for their world and their children. This is the calling of the Church. Necessity by the will of God requires it of us. However nicely religion lines things all up, if at the end of the day we have not bread, we have failed. There need be no fear that we will put other people out of business by an overproduction of bread. We each have our place where our bread is needed. Besides all this, there is an enemy who opposes bread making. Without the grace of God we will never produce bread in any generation. There are just too many problems and too many things to stop it. Proud people do not make bread. While we sit thinking of how great we must be, God is waiting for someone who is willing to make bread that He might feed the world. The world has not rejected Jesus as we think it has. What is being rejected is our image of Jesus, which we tell them is Jesus. Those who hunger for bread know better. "Thy King cometh unto thee: he is just, and having salvation; lowly, and riding upon an ass, and upon a colt the foal of an ass" (Zech. 9:9).

REPRESENTATION

Bread is a representation of the Body of Christ, and the Body of Christ itself is a representation of heavenly things. I want to look at one representation that the Body is, but first a look at representation itself.

The word *representation* has important meaning. Because of its importance, much assault has been made upon its meaning. Distortions seem to exert themselves at every turn. The word most commonly used in Christian circles to express representation is *symbolism*. It may well be in times past that symbolism has meant representation, but in our day it does not usually mean that. Whatever words are used, the importance is the ideas contained behind the words.

Jesus spoke often of Himself in representative language. "I am the vine and ye are the branches" (John 15:5). He did not mean that He was a literal vine in some vineyard that you could go and handle with your hands. Yet that literal vine in a real sense is a true representation of Jesus, not just a symbol of Him. You could take that vine in your hands and see the characteristics and functions of Christ. Therefore, it is a true representation of Christ, not just some foggy symbol of Him.

Jesus said, "I am the way" (John 14:6). Christ did not mean that He literally was a road found somewhere in this world, where you could go and touch the ground and say you have touched Jesus. Yet when we see a road we see in a true sense a representation of what He is, a way to God. In this sense the road is real in representation, not foggy as in symbolism.

Jesus said, "I am the door of the sheep" (John 10:7). This does not mean that a door in this world is Christ, but it does mean that Christ is a door to God. In this sense a door is representative in a real way of Christ. You can look at a door in a home or some shelter and see a true likeness of Jesus. But it is ludicrous to say that Christ meant that the door itself was He.

The apostle Paul in the same way used representative language to say, "Therefore we are buried with him by baptism into death" (Rom. 6:4). In representative language you cannot look at baptism and say, "I have died with Christ," simply on the basis of literal baptism, anymore than we can look at a door or a road and say I have literally touched Christ. Yet baptism in a real sense is a representation of what happens spiritually in our relationship with Christ. It is therefore real in that sense and not just a foggy symbol.

On the last night He spent with His disciples, Jesus broke the bread and said, "Take, eat, this is my body" (Matt. 26:26). He did not mean the bread in His hands was literally His flesh. Jesus meant that it represented His flesh. Or when Christ took the cup and said, "This is my blood of the New Testament" (Matt. 26:28), He did not mean the cup in His hands was literally His blood. Such a thing is not what Christ was speaking of; He meant that it represented His blood. But Christ also did not mean that the bread and the wine were simply vague or foggy symbols, as we understand symbolism. The wine and bread were true representations of what is Christ and His body.

Symbolism Defined

What symbolism often means to us is a concept that has its roots in idol worship, where the worshipers are uncertain of who or what their god is. That's why symbolism is forbidden to the people of God. God said, "Thou shalt not make unto thee any graven image, or any likeness of any thing that is in heaven above, or that is in the earth beneath, or that is in the water under the earth" (Exod. 20:4). Our meaning of symbolism usually means the same thing as a graven image. An idol, or a graven image, as it is called in this case, is not as we would think of a picture of say, a landscape or person. A picture or painting in our age, in its normal understanding, is a true picture or representation of what the landscape or person really is. It is not a symbol, all fuzzy and hazy, but a representation. When you look at the picture or painting you know what you are looking at.

As of late, things in the arts have deteriorated from clear-cut representation, into abstractions known as modern art. But modern art is in fact not modern at all, but quite ancient. It is symbolism, with fuzzy clouds rolling across the painting in ways they do not naturally do, and splotches of paint daubed at random and without order or structure onto the canvas. Feelings, not reality, are being expressed. It is symbolism. Sculpture awards are given for grotesque figures such as one in an exhibition at the Peninsula Fine Arts Center titled *Queen*. The figure has no resemblance to a queen in the common meaning of the word. It is in fact not intended to have any such resemblance, as that would be considered simplistic and naïve by those who consider themselves advanced and in the know. This is all not advanced at all but a regression into heathenism.

One can also follow the descent into symbolism in the use of statues of lions placed at the entrance of driveways or public buildings. Lions themselves are not symbols, as lions are real and by nature fierce, so one could expect them to perhaps guard buildings. The symbolism comes in when wings are added or eight toes or five tails. That is now symbolism, as it does not represent anything that really is but something as it is imagined to be, and what is being symbolized is not clearly known.

The apostle Paul traced the progress of symbolism, or idol making, in Romans chapter 1. Paul said that since the creation of the world the invisible things of God can be clearly seen, being understood by the things that are made. But that people, when they knew God by seeing those things, didn't glorify Him as God, nor were they thankful. They, instead, professed themselves to be wise, and so became fools and changed the glory of the incorruptible God into images made like corruptible man, birds, four-footed beasts, and creeping things (from verses 20–23). The images made were likenesses or symbols, not representations of man, birds, four-footed beasts, and creeping things. We have only to see the pictures or actually see an idol to fully understand this symbolism. They include distorted faces of men and animals, hideous masks of spirits, and unnamed other weird expressions of natural beings. Idols do not represent anything real; they symbolize the unreal. God said through David in the Old Testament, "Their idols are silver and gold, the work of men's hands. They have mouths, but they speak not: eyes have they, but they see not: They have ears, but they hear not: noses have they, but they smell not: They have hands, but they handle not: feet have they, but they walk not: neither speak they through their throat" (Ps. 115:4–7). The apostle Paul said, "What say I then? that the idol is any thing" (1 Cor. 10:19). Symbols are not real, but representations are real. That is why Jesus spoke of representations and not of symbols.

The apostle speaks of the result of misusing the natural, as God will give men and women up to perhaps the ultimate misuse of nature, that of lusting men for men and women for women (Rom. 1:27). We do not need to look that far down the road to see the results of symbolism. In our everyday lives, symbolizing an object will result in us losing the natural use of that object. Furniture was made for many uses, but how much is antique furniture really used? Representation does not always follow just appearance, though. Dolls were made to play with, but pretty ones often sit on the shelf while little girls play with the simple ones they like best. The rag dolls that look less like the real than the porcelain ones do, are better at representation and so better loved.

The path of symbolism follows the real to the unreal. We should be on our guard against this. Even things such as souvenirs and knickknacks sitting around the house can progress from something real to a symbol. That pair of cute carved kittens given by one's mother can progress from kittens to symbolism, till they are no longer kittens, but the love of one's mother, to be guarded and kept with great care. Souvenirs come to symbolize a whole trip, and the head of a game animal the entire adventure. So something real comes to mean something unreal.

This is no less true in the things of the Church. If we symbolize natural things God has given the Church to use, such as baptism, the bread and the wine, and the head veil of 1 Corinthians 11, we will lose the power of the things themselves to be of use to us. And so they will become what we have chosen for them to be, symbols without power.

Paul the apostle spoke of a woman who had power on her head (1 Cor. 11:10). This woman represents the Church and stands in contrast to the Church we are often familiar with, which does not have power. A Church without power is a Church that holds things in her hands that are only symbols.

The Church as a Representation

1 Corinthians 11:2–3

The apostle Paul spoke of an ordinance he had delivered to the church at Corinth. This was an ordinance rooted not just in the temporal, but in the heavenlies; not just for one group of people, but for the world. It was an ordinance established both in heaven and on earth. The ordinance is that man was a representation of Christ, that woman was a representation of man, and that Christ was the representation of God (1 Cor. 11:2–3).

This representation would be a real representation in the sense that it was tangible and seeable and not simply a symbol. It would apply to all nations, tongues, peoples, and races. Because of this ordinance, Paul said that any man anywhere in this world who prayed or prophesied with his head covered would misrepresent Christ and so dishonor Christ—because Christ is no longer covered but uncovered to the world (Eph. 3:2–6; also Col. 1:26–27). Colossians 1:26: "Even the mystery which hath been hid from ages and from generations, but now is made manifest to his saints: To whom God would make known what is the riches of the glory of this mystery among the Gentiles; which is Christ in you, the hope of glory. . . ." Any man now functioning in religious service to God with a covered head would be representing a covered Christ, and so dishonor Him.

In the Old Testament Christ was covered, as was the representation. Many godly men had long hair (Num. 6:5; Judg. 13:5; 1 Sam. 1:11) and covered their heads like the devout Jewish men who still wear caps today, representing an Old Testament "Christianity" (Lev. 10:6, 21:10). The beard in the Old Testament was also included in the long hair on the head of the man. Beards were the norm, with instructions given by Moses on not shaving off the corners of beards (Lev. 19:27, 21:5). The judgments and wrath of God included consuming, cutting off, and clipping the beards of men (Isa. 7:20, 15:2; Jer. 48:37). Other references attest to the commonality of a full-length beard in activities of war, disease, and normal everyday life. Ezra spoke of rending his mantle and garment and plucking off hairs from his head and beard at the arrival of bad news (Ezra 9:3). Hair must be of considerable length before it lends itself to handy plucking. When the ambassadors of David were sent to Hanun, the son of Nahash, Hanun tormented them by shaving off half their beards and cutting off half their garments. David told his men to wait at Jericho until their beards had grown back, again showing the value placed on the beard in the Old Testament (2 Sam. 10:1–5).

There is a double representation throughout the first part of 1 Corinthians 11 as Paul speaks on this matter. The representation is both in the natural state of things and in the response that men and women can have. The natural state men and women have without asking for it, while the covered or uncovered head is the response that men and women can choose to have. Paul goes on to show that long hair that covers the head is its own representation of the natural state of the man and woman. He shows that nature itself teaches us that long hair is unbecoming to a man but becoming to a woman. There is then the response that a man or woman can have to the natural representation, and that is to cover or uncover the head itself. This is the representation of headship. The natural representation of the long hair in itself only bears witness to the covered or uncovered head of the man or woman. It is the covered and uncovered head that has spiritual significance, although both representations have universal meaning and understanding, for they are rooted in ordinance. God has so established it.

Long hair has meaning for both the man and the woman. It represents a natural strength and glory. That glory on the head of man in the Old Testament was no shame, as Christ was yet covered. The men of the Old Testament, therefore, had long hair, long beards, and covered their heads in religious service. They also were fleet of foot, strong of arm, good with the sword, and bore other characteristics of men who walk in their own glory and strength. That was acceptable and so ordained at that time by the ordinance that was in heaven, for Christ was not yet revealed. Now that Christ is revealed, we have changed, but the ordinance has not changed, for the same ordinance is being followed. That ordinance is Christ. We are simply following the heavenly pattern whether Christ is covered or uncovered.

1 Corinthians 11:4

So the apostle—dealing with both representations, the hair and the veil—says that any man praying or prophesying with his head covered dishonors his head (1 Cor. 11:4). By either having long hair or covering his head with a veil while praying or prophesying, a man misrepresents Christ and so dishonors Christ. This is not a certain church principle or something belonging to any particular denomination. It is a universal principle. It is universal also in that many religions that have a covered Christ wear the head veiled by their church leaders in religious service. Why do the pope and cardinals of the Catholic Church wear skullcaps? How do Muslims know about veiling the head of the man? Who taught them that? The Jew has carried it over from the Old Testament, but what of ancient lands containing the Kingdom of Mustang, as reported by *Reader's Digest*, October 1997, with its demon-chasing lamas and castles in the sky? How do they know to wear caps on the heads of their priests? They know it because it is a universal principle. It is an ordinance established in the heavenlies that man represents (or misrepresents) Christ by covering or uncovering his head in religious service to God. So, it is of value to note that many religions that do not have a revealed and uncovered Christ follow the principle and cover the heads of their religious leaders. Also note that the context of the 1 Corinthians passage where Paul deals with this subject does not pertain only to a church service but wherever prayer and prophesying is done.

1 Corinthians 11:5

Likewise, dealing with both representations, any woman who cuts her hair or does not veil it while praying or prophesying dishonors her head (1 Cor. 11:5). She dishonors the man by misrepresenting the man as uncovered. It is now Christ who is to be seen, not us, as Christ is uncovered and not mankind. This covering of man can be taken in its most basic form to mean that our sins, shortcomings, and errors are to be covered by Christ and hidden from the view of the world. In the Church, love is to be the hallmark, and love provides a covering where sin can be dealt with honestly (Prov. 10:12). The covering of man means also to cover the strength and glory of man. How many churches have the first one right in that they represent the uncovering of Christ, but they do not deal with the second, the covering of the faults of their brother or of the glory and strength of man? We dishonor ourselves as Christians when we are proud and arrogant and show to the world our strengths, accomplishments, achievements, and noteworthiness. It is Christianity of all places that should be clothed with humility, for does God not resist the proud but give grace to the humble (1 Pet. 5:5)?

It could be noted that churches in which men cover their heads, either by the cap or veil, also often require veils for women. The distinction is that the veil is no longer just a veil but a religious object, whether in style, form, make, color, or excessive size. Some mark is used to make the veil on the women religious and therefore useful to their own religious ends—going well beyond its simple use of covering the hair.

1 Corinthians 11:6

The apostle Paul then proceeds to say after verse five that any woman desiring not to wear the veil in the context of praying and prophesying should cut off her long hair. But he adds that since it is a shame for a woman to cut off her long hair, let her wear the veil. Again Paul is using both the hair and the veil as being representative of the principle. In the hair we have been given the principle whether we like or not, and in the veil we have a choice in the matter. Paul says that it is a shame for a woman to cut her hair. That is a principle rooted in human nature. Not so long ago the sense of regret was still with women when they cut their hair for the first time, and it still lies there, though unremembered. Any woman who returns to it, though she may not have thought of it since her childhood, will find the natural instinct still there and quite her own.

1 Corinthians 11:7

Verse seven of 1 Corinthians 11 serves as a short summary in repeating that man is the image and glory of God and so should not cover his head, either with long hair or a veil. Women on the other hand, being the glory of the man, should cover their heads with long hair and then cover that glory with a veil, that the glory of man both should exist and be hidden (1 Cor. 11:7). From the latter part of this verse comes this principle: as the woman's glory (her long hair) is only for her husband, covered from the sight of other men, so the Church also has her glory, covered from the eyes of the world. Again this principle is rooted in universal nature, as the world has an expression for it. A loose woman morally is known as "letting down her hair."

The Contrast—1 Corinthians 11:8–12

Paul then gives an amazing lesson in humility and order that often is missed by many in Christianity. He supplies an account of the beauty of the interconnection and interlocking of God's creation and order, how one is not created without the other. Paul does this by using the natural order of things: 1) how man was not created from a woman, and yet is born of a woman and so does not exist without her; 2) how a woman was created from a man in the Garden of Eden, and yet from that day on has been the means of bringing more men into the world. Both do not exist by themselves but as all things they exist from God. In the middle of this, Paul places verse ten, which says that for this reason a woman ought to have power on her head, because of the angels. The mystery and depth of that verse is seen in representation, for Paul speaks not just of a woman but what she represents, the Church (1 Cor. 11:8–12).

If we read those verses (1 Cor. 11:8–12), placing the representative word in place of man or woman, we still get a correct reading and see the greater depth of what Paul meant. Man represents Christ, and Christ can be placed where we read *man*. The woman represents man or the Church, and so *Church* can be placed where we read *woman*.

Reading with Representation

For Christ is not of the church, but the church is of Christ. Neither was Christ created for the church, but the church for Christ. For this cause ought the church to have power on her head because of the angels. Nevertheless neither is Christ without the church, neither the church without Christ in the LORD. For as the Church is of Christ, even so is Christ also by the church, but all things of God (1 Cor. 11:8–12).

It should be no wonder to us that Paul would say that for this reason the Church should have power on her head, as she lives in this position because of the ministry of the angels. Hebrews says that angels are all ministering spirits sent forth to minister to them who shall be heirs of salvation (Heb. 1:14). This is power indeed, but it belongs to those believers who are in the correct position, not to those with the correct programs, ministries, or other criteria.

Paul's Test

Paul then concludes his arguments by appealing to our natural judgment (1 Cor. 11:13–16). The question is whether it is in order for a woman to pray to God unveiled. To answer this question, Paul proposes that we put the question to the test of nature. Let us bring in a man without religious background and training and let him judge. What does this man know by nature?

Place before this man, with only his nature to guide him, a man with long hair. Will he not say that long hair on this man standing before him is distasteful, or as Paul says, "a shame"? The answer of course is yes. Let us then place before this man without religious background or training a woman with long hair. Is it distasteful to him? The answer of course is no, it is not distasteful, but as Paul says, "a glory" (1 Cor. 11:13–15).

So according to the test does not nature itself teach us that a man with long hair is out of order? For with long hair he is covered and ought not to be. The long hair is therefore not the end in itself, but a universal witness that a man ought not to cover his head with a material covering. So also according to the test, nature teaches us that if a woman has long hair it is a glory to her and not a shame, for with long hair she is covered and ought so to be. The long hair is therefore not an end in itself, but a universal witness that a woman ought to cover her head with a material covering. For there it is written by the glory of long hair in a woman, both that it is a glory to be covered, and that the glory should be covered. By nature, the implication is given and the impulse is in both the man and the woman. In the man the instinct is to uncover his head, and in the women the instinct to cover her head and its glory from the eyes around her (1 Cor. 11:13–15).

1 Corinthians 11:16

The apostle thus brings his arguments to a satisfactory conclusion and says further if any man still wants to argue about this, that he has no such custom, neither do the churches of God (1 Cor. 11:16). That was good enough for Paul and seems like it should be good enough for us too. We ought to be, whether we are or not, a Church that does not seek to exalt her seat above the stars or to climb the north side of the mountain of God as Satan did (Isa. 14:13), but to be one that dwells under the shadow of the Almighty (Ps. 91:1). Ought that Church not indeed have power on her head?

We find then in representation a gauge that can be used as Christians on where we are at as individuals and as a Church. Whether we like it or not, representation gives a glimpse into the state of things. Take baptism for example. Just because a church baptizes an individual, it cannot be guaranteed that salvation is granted, for baptism is representation. But if a church does not baptize, it would say much about the condition of that church, because of the issues which baptism represents—the death and burial of Christ, the resurrection and entering in of the new life of

God. The practice of the representation and the belief are connected. I know that some in church history have tried to separate the two, but they cannot be separated.

In the same way the covered and the uncovered head of the man and women speaks in representation of spiritual beliefs, which are larger than the mere practice of covering and uncovering the head. Just because the practice of covering and uncovering the head is done or attempted, does not guarantee that the spiritual belief has been achieved anymore than baptism can guarantee the saving of the soul. But the church that does not practice the representation speaks much to its condition in respect to the things that the practice represents. This is inescapable as far as I can see.

THE BREAD

With that we come to the end of the process. This is the story of bread making. There are deeper meanings to walking with God than we may have thought. Back when we first started, God placed in our hearts the longings for a harvest, and then began preparing our hearts for the seed to grow. We marveled to see His hand at work. From the first beginnings of breadmaking we took joy in new life and new growth, enthralled with all He was doing. Our hearts became lost in the beauty of the harvest, and we thought it would always be so. But God had much more in store for us than we could then imagine. His thoughts are not our thoughts, and His ways are not our ways. Lessons awaited us on the order, structure, and will of God. Heaven wants bread to feed the world, even as Jesus Himself was bread, and this requires a long process.

It takes a brave soul to venture with God beyond the success and prosperity of the harvest. Those who do are those who have learned to love the truth, not just as a fact in some catechism but as a man. For now Truth has become a man and walks with us. One of the names of Jesus is Emmanuel, which is interpreted *"God with us"* (Matt. 1:23). This is fundamental to Christianity. We are not to walk alone in our journeys but to go with God.

After the harvest God continues to lead us, and we find that even that which is born in us from above must be refined and purified. The chaff must fall away. Who is up to these things? The failure, the crushing, the fire, and the brokenness have no meaning to us in this life unless we have learned the values of another world. The values of this world teach us to hold on and let nothing go, but God would remove the chaff and have us whole. He would have us pure. Does not purity require the removal of all elements other than the one we are after? If we want gold, then all the other minerals, even though they have value, must be removed. When we are finished and the gold is purified, we have less to work with, but it has more value then it did before it was purified. More can now be done with less. Holiness also consists of purity. The harvest is not yet whole—it is the bread that is whole. We are made holy as we are moved beyond the harvest, through threshing, failure, crushing, and the fire. Only then are we made pure or whole.

If we are to become holy or whole, we must learn that God is safe. Making God unsafe is perhaps among the greatest violence that religion has done to the concept of holiness. Religion has made men afraid of God. When we are in sin, then without doubt we should know fear, for the fear of the LORD is the beginning of wisdom. Yet if God had intended that we shake in our boots every time we think of Him, would He not have continued to speak from the top of a mountain burning with fire and trembling with His glory, so that we would be properly afraid? We should all know that this is not what has happened. As the writer of Hebrews says, *"For ye are not come unto the mount that might be touched, and that burned with fire, nor unto blackness, and darkness, and tempest"* (Heb. 12:18). When Jesus came He told us about the Father, not about some mountain burning with a tempest and blackness. As leaders and teachers of believers, we must not make God an unsafe place to be. Already in the Old Testament the lesson was there for anyone to see, if man had not been bent on misunderstanding. When God told Moses to take off his shoes at the burning bush in the desert, it was not to demand some sign of reverence but to establish a basis of reality for their conversation. God seeks to establish that same basis in our lives. Our shoes are for protection, because the desert is a dangerous place to walk. That is why Moses was wearing shoes, and that is why God told him to take them off. God was saying to Moses, *I will not talk to you until you take off your protection, because with me even in the desert all is safe.* If Moses had not taken off his shoes, the conversation with God at the burning bush would not have continued. So it is with us. A man does not get far with God with his shoes on. With God all is safe because He is holy. With Him it is safe even in the desert, and we must take off our shoes and trust Him.

In the desert we also find out where our heart is. How convinced are we that if things were just easier we would do all right? Will we go on blaming our shortcomings on our hard life, or will we face the truth that even if we lived in the Garden of Eden, we would still fail? Since Adam and

Eve fell, all are fallen. Are we better than they? We can no longer live in the Garden, for it has been closed to man. Now we walk through the desert, where the last Adam, Jesus Christ, gained for us the final victory. There in the desert, in the place of hunger and thirst and cold, the gateway to Heaven was opened by the victory of Jesus. Religious leaders may gather men unto themselves with promises of religious comforts, but alone in the desert, the Son of Man leads the way to hope and redemption.

Another lesson we must learn is to lay up our treasures in heaven and not on this earth. Are we disappointed if the world doesn't notice our testimonies, experiences, gifts, and good works? Or must everything that happens to us in Christianity have its immediate reward? If we want recognition, then we are laying up our treasures on this earth. Those who walk with God learn to lay up their treasures in heaven, for they believe they are the representation in this world of things to come. We are not yet what we are to be, but we carry that representation within us, as the baby is carried in the mother's womb. In the womb, the baby has hands that aren't yet useful, feet that do not walk, eyes that see but dimly, and a mouth that does not yet speak. As the child in that surreal darkness, so we also are being formed for another world. God doesn't give us experiences to brag about to anyone who will listen, but to prepare us for eternity. As does the baby, we will awake one morning in another land we know little about. Will we have spent our time only in what seems useful in this earthly world? Or have we been growing legs, arms, and eyes that at times seem out of place in this world but will find their use over there? As a baby born into this world knows his mother's voice though he never saw his mother before, those who have laid up their treasures in heaven will awake in wonder to the sound of the same voice that called them into being, heard so often, dimly and faraway across the waters of time and space, calling them into life eternal.

If we have not learned it already, we will learn then how to be bread. For the Master Himself will set the table and serve. He said He would not partake of the table again until He sat down anew in the kingdom of His Father. *"For I say unto you, I will not any more eat thereof, until it be fulfilled in the kingdom of God"* (Luke 22:16). There the Son honors the Father, the Father honors the Son, and we are called brethren. Should we not prepare to be with Him, though He tarries long and the shadows lengthen? For we must be bread.

PART TWO—

HINDRANCES TO BREAD MAKING

There Is a Will of God

7

Perhaps the greatest hindrances to bread making are the false concepts regarding the will of God for believers. If Christianity is to be anything, we must return to the belief that there is a will of God along with the liberty to do that will. If we are not clear on the issues related to the will of God, much confusion will result, leading many into hopelessness. We talk in our church theology about whether or not a person has the power to do the will of God. That is not the heart of the matter. The heart is spiritual growth. If we do not first grow, then in the end we will not be able to do anything. A child first must grow strong legs before he or she can run. We do need power, but the power is needed, as the apostle said, *"To become the sons of God"* (John 1:12). As the bird hatched from the egg needs power to become a bird, not just a nestling, so we need power to become sons, and not just children in the sense of the Law. We need power to grow beyond tutors and governors (Gal. 4:1, 2). After that, though, the issue is not one of power but of freedom.

After it is grown the bird needs freedom to fly in the air, and after he is a son, the son of God needs liberty in which to live. The question is not, then, whether we have the power, but whether we have the liberty.

Liberty is needed to do the will of God; the power should have been expended in becoming the sons of God. Too much of the Church has it all turned around. Either there are no tutors and governors, or if there are, they keep telling us how to do the will of God and not how to become sons of God. That is like telling nestlings to fly and then, when they quite naturally fall to the ground, telling them they must stay in the nest. It has always been that when men or women understand the will of God, their first concern is not whether they have the power to do that will but whether they have the liberty. When a man or woman talks of doing the will of God, and their first concern is the lack of power, they are as a nestling being pushed to fly by some man. Men for their own gain try to push people along in whatever direction they want them to go. We must not be one of those. God wants to plant within us a deep, constant desire for growth, and when it is time to do the will of God, our desire, put in us by God Himself, will be for freedom. The apostle spoke not of desire for power but for freedom: "*Withal praying also for us, that God would open unto us a door of utterance, to speak the mystery of Christ, for which I am also in bonds*" (Col. 4:3). How will the Church be what she is to be if she does not give liberty? Or if she is not willing to take the fallen to the One who can provide the power to become a son?

The record of the Church is not good on these issues. It often makes martyrs of those who insist on freedom to live the will of God. The martyrs of the Church die for freedom, not for power. On the contrary, those who die for power to do what they want are in king's houses and the halls of government, not in the Church. The true Church has always been about transforming men and women into sons and daughters of God, and fostering the freedom to do the will of God. Where there is no liberty there really is no Church—just an organization patterned after the world. If we refuse correct doctrine on this subject, our people either will conclude that there really is no way to know the will of God or will labor under constant burdens they cannot carry.

A long time ago the young king Rehoboam sought advice on how to govern his new kingdom after the people had come to him with this request: "Thy father made our yoke grievous: now therefore ease thou somewhat the grievous servitude of thy father, and his heavy yoke that he put upon us, and we will serve thee" (2 Chron. 10:4).

When the young king sought the advice of the old men of his kingdom, they said: "*If thou be kind to this people, and please them, and speak good words to them, they will be thy servants for ever*" (2 Chron. 10:7).

But the young men of his kingdom said quite the opposite: "*Thus shalt thou answer the people that spake unto thee, saying, Thy father made our yoke heavy, but make thou it somewhat lighter for us; thus shalt thou say unto them, My little finger shall be thicker than my father's loins. For whereas my father put a heavy yoke upon you, I will put more to your yoke: my father chastised you with whips, but I will chastise you with scorpions*" (2 Chron. 10:10–11).

The story goes on to say that the king chose the advice of the young men over the old and split his kingdom. This is not just the story of a young king, but a story of choices that are still being made by men today. Jesus spoke of religious leaders, "*For they bind heavy burdens and grievous to be borne, and lay them on men's shoulders; but they them-selves will not move them with one of their fingers*" (Matt. 23:4).

It is an old problem. When there is a need or a deficit in believers, do we side with taxes and burdens, or do we side with growth? Taxes and burdens may seem to solve some problems in the short term, but growth will produce lasting results in the long term. Growth produces believers who are capable of greater output, while taxes and burdens take away even the little they have and spend it on the cause, or the church, or whatever else is in vogue right then.

Obedience or Sacrifice

Many may be surprised to find out there is a big difference between obedience and sacrifice. Early in the Old Testament God already had to deal with man's tendency to prefer sacrifice over obedience. God Himself had instituted and commanded the sacrifices of the Law, but in the end, the heart of God found no pleasure in them, because of what man had done with sacrifices. "*Above when he said, Sacrifice and offering and burnt offerings and offering for sin thou wouldest not, neither hadst pleasure therein; which are offered by the law. . . .*" (Heb. 10:8).

Even though God had commanded sacrifices in the Old Testament, Jesus spoke not of sacrifices, but spoke of loving God and one's neighbor as oneself. "*And to love him with all the heart, and with all the understanding, and with all the soul, and with all the strength, and to love his neighbour as himself, is more than all whole burnt offerings and sacrifices*" (Mark 12:33).

The apostle Paul spoke not of sacrifices in the old sense, but spoke of a living sacrifice versus a dead one. "*I beseech you therefore, brethren, by the mercies of God, that ye present your bodies a living sacrifice, holy, acceptable unto God, which is your reasonable service*" (Rom. 12:1).

The apostle Peter spoke not of the old fleshly sacrifices but of a new spiritual one. "*Ye also, as lively stones, are built up a spiritual house, an holy priesthood, to offer up spiritual sacrifices, acceptable to God by Jesus Christ*" (1 Pet. 2:5).

It is now a new life that we live in Christ Jesus. Gone is the old concept of offering your sacrifice in fear. The generations that did not obey but gave a little of what they had to get by are to be no more. Failure to distinguish between obedience to God that always is based in liberty, and sacrifice that is based in timidity and cowardice, is to greatly hinder bread making. The apostle Paul said, "*God has not given us the spirit of fear*" (2 Tim. 1:7).

The Church ought to be one place where there are no sacrifices—a place where men do not grovel. Sacrifice, as man has made it, belongs to cowards at heart. It is to appease an angry deity that children are offered on altars of fire. The heathen sacrifice to get rain and dew on their crops, and much of Christianity is little better. How tragic that much of church organization is geared toward sacrifice and not obedience, making little differentiation between the two and presenting sacrifice as obedience to God. The Roman Catholic Church has the most obvious examples, with its "Hail Mary's" and other exercises prescribed as penance for sins. Obedience is not even an aim, as the Church officially teaches that we all sin in word, thought, or deed each day. Whether or not we sin somewhere every day by weaknesses, or faults, or oversights is really not the point—most people have little interest or energy to go into the technical arguments of that subject. The point is that the Church should lift its people out of the gutter of sinning and sacrifice, for the two revolve around each other. Jesus said, *"Go, and sin no more"* (John 8:11). So it is possible, at least when dealing with a specific sin, to cease from sinning.

The timid and cowardly sacrifice because they are not obeying. Sacrifice is man's solution to a heart that has failed to obey. Wherever you find a man sacrificing, you will find a man who is disobeying.

King Saul

The first example in the Old Testament is King Saul. The prophet Samuel finds the king coming back from his assigned job of totally destroying the Amalekites. The king greets the prophet with the words, *"I have performed the commandments of the LORD"* (1 Sam. 15:13–23). Those who sacrifice somehow in their own way believe they have done the will of God. Samuel responds with the obvious question, *"What meaneth then this bleating of the sheep in mine ears, and the lowing of the oxen which I hear?"* That is the obvious question all who sacrifice must face. If you have done the commandments of God, why are those commandments not done?

The king then tells the prophet in essence that he has come up with a better plan than God's. For he was afraid to face the people, who didn't like what God had said. So we see that timidity is a driving force behind sacrifice. Saul planned to let the people disobey and spare the best animals, but then to have them sacrifice the animals to God. He argued that in the end the animals would be destroyed and God's will would be done. Many church leaders reason exactly the same way. Afraid to require the will of God of the people in obedience, they plan to later require the will of God in sacrifice and expect that to be the same thing.

The prophet Samuel thought otherwise and told the king so. "When thou wast little in thine own sight, wast thou not made head of the tribes of Israel, and the LORD anointed thee king over Israel?" (1 Samuel 15:17). In other words, when the king thought lowly of himself, he could obey, but when he began to think he was somebody, he lost the ability to obey and began to plot his own ways to do what God said to do. That is just like we are. Isaiah 53:6 says, "*We have turned every one to his own way*." Doing things our own way in obeying God is just as much sin as doing things our own way in the world.

Samuel told Saul: Are your sacrifices and burnt offerings as pleasing to God as obeying his voice? "*Behold, to obey is better than sacrifice, and to hearken than the fat of rams*." Samuel went on to say that sacrificing was really rebellion, or doing things your own way, and was no different than what the witches were doing. Disobedience is no different than idol worship or any other iniquity, even when followed by sacrifice.

Sacrificing snuffs out the precious air of liberty and confines the soul of a man to the nest with his own doings, until the sight of his pale, stunted self is a horror to the man himself. We see this path as it is followed by King Saul. Later, after sacrificing instead of obeying, Saul was tormented by evil spirits, and at the end driven by his own fear to a witch for advice and died later on the battlefield at the point of his own sword (1 Sam. 28:5, 31:4).

Isaiah and Jeremiah

Even in the Old Testament God began to deal with sacrifices. In Isaiah 1:10–20, many things used for sacrifice that had grown sacred to men were shown to have little value to God. The LORD asked the leaders of Israel what was the purpose of a multitude of sacrifices. He was full of their burnt offerings of rams and of the fat of fed beasts and had no delight in the blood of bullocks, lambs, or he-goats.

Now we may think that has nothing to do with us, since we no longer sacrifice animals. But it does. It is the nature of sacrifice itself that concerns God, no matter what kind of sacrifice it is. God asks the children of Israel, "*When ye come to appear before me, who hath required this at your hand, to tread my courts?*" That would be like asking us, "Who has told you to come to church?"

"*Bring no more vain oblations*" speaks of gifts and offerings to God. That certainly could apply to us. "*Incense is an abomination unto me.*" While that may not apply to some, there are churches who still use literal incense in services; and for the rest of us, do not our actions sometimes look a little like someone trying to work up a good smell to God? God is really saying to His people, why do you try to clean up and smell good with religious actions when your hearts are unclean? Do you think that will be pleasing to God? Would it not be better to obey?

"*The new moons and sabbaths, the calling of assemblies, the appointed feasts . . .*" God says to do away with these because they are iniquity. Even the solemn meeting the soul of God hates. They are a trouble to Him, and He grows weary of bearing them. What does all this mean? Does God want no more gatherings of His people? What distresses God is the use that we make of meetings as sacrifices to Him—how we honor meetings, gatherings, and appointed times in the hope they will cleanse us from sin. You think these Scriptures have no relevance to our lives? Look around and ask yourself how much hope we place in retreats, weekend meetings, conferences, special gatherings, and scheduled speakers. In the solemn meeting we go and reverently listen to some special speaker tell us all about how to live Christianity. We are pressured to place great confidence in that as a corrective measure in our Christian lives. We live like you know what, and then to make things right, we sacrifice an appointed meeting or a series of meetings. That is the kind of thing God says to do away with. He is tired of it.

God says further, "*When ye spread forth your hands, I will hide mine eyes from you.*" The Charismatic and Pentecostal people act at times as if they themselves discovered raising hands. In reality it was done a long time ago. Here in the Old Testament God says He will hide His eyes from people who sacrifice before Him with raised hands in worship. Does that mean God is against raising hands? No. It means God is against the confidence that men place in raised hands as a cleanser for sin. You may say that is ridiculous and would never happen, but it is nevertheless true. There are places where it is not love that covers a multitude of sins but raised hands that cover a multitude of sins. All you have to do is raise your hands in worship and you are regarded as a holy man. That is the kind of attitude God is against. Sacrifice does not make us holy.

Why not just obey? Because sacrifice is easier.

"*When ye make many prayers, I will not hear.*" God is not against praying, but He is against praying as a means of being clean while our hands are full of blood. Instead of offering prayers as a sacrifice in church, we ought to go and make ourselves clean from our sins and the evil of our doings by ceasing from evil. How much religious exercise in church is a cover-up for unholy living? We would be shocked if we knew. Some of the sacrificing in church that impresses us so much does not impress God at all.

God says that instead of sacrificing we ought to go and learn to do well. Now really, how many people are going to be impressed with me if that is all I do? Just do well. That doesn't make much of a splash at testimony time—"I was out learning to do well." You get the point.

We are to seek judgment. That does not mean to be church troublemakers, whining about what your church is buying or what color the Sunday school room is. It means caring about the oppressed, those people who cannot help you back or advance your position in the eyes of men. It means to care about orphans and widows who are often taken advantage of. That is what God means by judgment.

Holiness is much less glamorous than we think. The LORD says, *"Come now and let us reason together"*—that is, reason together about our sacrifices that are doing no good. The LORD can take and do with our sins that are as scarlet what sacrifices cannot, and make them white as snow; though they be red like crimson, they can be made by God as wool. It is God who has the power to make sons of God, and we should leave that business to Him, or go to Him for it. It takes liberty from sacrifices to both grow in and do the will of God.

Jeremiah said, *"There is no use now in burning sweet incense from Sheba before me! Keep your expensive perfumes! I cannot accept your offerings; they have no sweet fragrance for me. The LORD of Hosts, the God of Israel says, away with your offerings and sacrifices! It wasn't offerings and sacrifices I wanted from your fathers when I led them out of Egypt. That was not the point of my command. But what I told them was: obey me and I will be your God and you shall be my people; only do as I say and all shall be well!"* (Jer. 6:20, 7:21–23, TLB). What is the lesson for us? Is it not the same as it was for the Israelites? Do we not also remember, if we pause to think, when we were first born again? Like the Israelites we were lead out of Egypt, not thinking of sacrifices but yearning for freedom to obey God. But now all the religious stuff has pulled our hearts away. What with meetings, obligations, Bible reading, devotional time, prayer time, and books on marriage and family, where are we? Have we lost the freedom to fly, to obey God?

The Minor Prophets

On the issue of sacrifices Hosea says—and note that this is still the Old Testament, even though it sounds like the New—"*For I desired mercy, and not sacrifice; and the knowledge of God more than burnt offerings*" (Hos. 6:6). Aren't religious people some of the most merciless people there are? Religious wars have been among the cruelest on Earth. The Crusades, the Inquisition, the slaughter of the Huguenots in France, and the Moslem jihad are but a few of many that could be named. Church history is red with the blood of its own people. And even during eras not apt to use the sword, there is little like opposing religious factions to stir up the exterminating instinct in the heart of men who consider themselves holy. God says He desires mercy and not sacrifice and knowledge of Him more than burnt offerings. Is that what our religious service does? Is it geared toward knowing more of God, or is it focused on offerings to man or God? Jesus said that to know God is eternal life (John 17:3).

Amos says it again: "*I hate your show and pretense—your hypocrisy of 'honoring' me with your religious feasts and solemn assemblies. I will not accept your burnt offerings and thank offerings. I will not look at your offerings of peace. Away with your hymns of praise—they are mere noise to my ears. I will not listen to your music, no matter how lovely it is. I want to see a mighty flood of justice—a torrent of doing good*" (Amos 5:21–24, TLB). The King James Version says, "*Let judgment run down as water, and righteousness as a mighty stream."* That is what God wants from His people, not hypocrisy and pretense. Even the old hymns sacred to so many God will not accept in the absence of justice and righteousness.

No sacrifice can take the place of a humble heart free to do the will of God. Micah 6:6–8 says further, *"Wherewith shall I come before the* LORD, *and bow myself before the high God? shall I come before him with burnt offerings, with calves of a year old? Will the lord be pleased with thousands of rams, or with ten thousands of rivers of oil? shall I give my firstborn for my transgression, the fruit of my body for the sin of my soul? He hath shewed thee, O man, what is good; and what doth the* LORD *require of thee, but to do justly, and to love mercy, and to walk humbly with thy God."*

Why do we not understand? Why does the Church pursue its own pleasure instead of the works of God? Because we are so bent on the attention and praise of men. Man can work himself into an absolute religious frenzy. If you do not believe that, read that cry in Micah again. This is made by a religious man full of passion: *"Shall I give my firstborn for my transgression, the fruit of my body for the sin of my soul?"* Why, such devotion would be welcome in many churches. We may not have child offerings any longer, but we have preachers who travel all over this world neglecting their children and considering it a sacrifice to God—while all the while God is saying, all I want is that you do justly, love mercy, and walk humbly with me. Why do we not do that instead of sacrifice? Because it is much harder. It is much, much more difficult for the man traveling the world ministering to others to instead stay home and minister to his family. So he prefers to sacrifice his family and minister to the world.

When we come to the New Testament we find the old concept of sacrifice gone. The apostle speaks now of a living sacrifice (Rom. 12:1). That is different. Now a man or woman offers sacrifice by living. The new living sacrifice is like a bird in the morning sitting on his tree limb pouring out his song. The bird does not have to strain or struggle to offer his morning song, but from deep within of what he is, a songbird, he offers a joyous tune of joy to the world. That is a living sacrifice.

When we do our religious service to God such as that, then we will know it is a living, and not a dead, sacrifice.

There Is the Real 8

Have we ever despaired of finding truth in this world? Most of us no doubt have. Yet it would do us well to remember that though we never meet an honest man, there are honest men; though we never meet a man of integrity, there are men of integrity; though we never find a church that has no pretense, there is the true Church. The presence of the false often hinders or discourages us from believing in the true. If we wish to make bread, then what our eyes see around us must not be allowed to interfere with our faith in the hand of God working among men. It is a little known secret that the presence of the false confirms the existence of the true. Many men have found the light because of the great darkness they have walked in demanded it. But how does the real start? It does not start with the natural realm, as sacrificing teaches.

It is a false promise and a false gospel that begins with the natural and moves toward spirituality. The true gospel makes us spiritual first and then moves to the natural.

Prayer, for example, involves the use of the natural. You bow your head, bend the knee, and assume other natural postures, and you say words. "Well," you may say, "of course there is natural praying, but there is also spiritual praying, and that is what I am doing." That kind of thinking is exactly what keeps getting us into trouble. The fact that we constantly have to make these natural things spiritual just shows that we ourselves are not spiritual. A spiritual man does not do spiritual praying in the sense that his prayer is much different than anyone else's. The prayers of a spiritual man are quite natural prayers, of the same kind used by everyone else. They are spiritual because he is spiritual. He is not spiritual because his prayers are spiritual. What we want to do is begin with the natural, the prayers, and make them spiritual. God wants to begin with the man and make him spiritual, and then when the man prays his prayers are spiritual, and so God has moved from the spiritual to the natural, and the natural is now spiritual. Any gospel or religion that goes the other way is false.

God does not require of us prayer or other good works and from our praying and good works move us into heavenly places. For when we were dead in sins, we were quickened by grace and raised up together and made to sit in heavenly places in Christ Jesus. For we are first His workmanship created in Christ Jesus and from there unto good works (Eph. 2:5–6,10).

With God the movement is not from the natural to the spiritual, but from the spiritual to the natural. God first gives and then expects a harvest. The devil, on the other hand, first asks of us a sacrifice and then promises a spiritual reward. You will get little bread making done if your religious activity comes not from your heart. Time will be wasted doing things for God, expecting Him to respond with rewards or increased growth. The life and river of God are free to all who ask and believe. Doing outward religious actions for men to see could be only an imitation of the real life with God that is lacking inside of you. Such lies lived do much damage to anyone who desires bread making, first and foremost to the one who practices them and also to those around that person.

How real, really, is your life with God? Do you live in a world where your spiritual thoughts and beliefs seem so real to you, but they never quite become reality? Or do you live in a world where your real practices—Bible reading, prayers, and fasting—never quite seem to produce much spiritual life? Both speak of a lack of the life of God.

It is important which direction you are moving in or trying to move in. The life of God has the power to move from the spiritual to the natural. There was once a Baby born in a manger who was God and became a Man, and from that time all spirits, according to the apostle John, are to be judged by their confession of whether this was true and whether it still is true (John 4:1–3). Do we really believe that spirituality can become flesh, or are we still trying to make flesh spiritual? These matters are of great importance if we desire to become bread.

The Garden of Eden

When Adam fell in the Garden, he fell to the offer of spirituality by the route of natural means. "Eat," said the devil, "ye shall be as gods" (Exod. 3:5). By eating, Adam and Eve caused the fall of man. In that fall they did gain the goal of becoming like the gods who know what is good and evil, but also they became like those gods in that they were cut off from life, or as Genesis records it, from *"the tree of life.*" God Himself said, "*Behold, the man is become as one of us, to know good and evil*" (Gen. 3:22). Jesus said in John 10:34: "*Is it not written in your law, I said, Ye are gods?*" Now man was like the fallen gods in that he could know right from wrong, but he could not live it. This is always the case with spirituality gained by natural means. You may know what is right, but you cannot live it.

The promise made by the serpent was a lie and still is. Adam chose his place at the tree of knowledge of good and evil and he got it, but he lost his place at the tree of life. So now also mankind knows so much and can do so little about it. Even the food man eats—that he must force to grow out of the ground by the sweat of his brow—never quite satisfies. With three meals a day he still gets hungry. And at the end, even with a lifetime of good eating and hours spent around the aroma and taste of delicious food, even after all those promises that food made to him, he still dies, for the tree of life was taken from him. This is the curse upon mankind in things approached from the natural.

Are we like that in our spiritual life? Do we now have the power to know good and evil, but not the power to do much about it? Such a man may be eating but he is not living. Are you like that? Do you know about the clothes a Christian should wear, and how he should pray, but you are still dying on the inside? Jesus came that we might live first and then do good works, for He is the tree of life.

John 6:35: "*And Jesus said unto them, I am the bread of life: he that cometh to me shall never hunger; and he that believeth on me shall never thirst.*"

This redemption Jesus brought is true spirituality and begins inward, pushing outward to the body. Out of the Spirit of God comes the visible. The other approach begins with the natural and promises to move in, but it never does.

The natural is called spirituality too, but is not rooted in truth. It is a lie, just as it was a lie that Eve would be better off by eating the apple. Yet this promise is made all the time to Christian people. Prayer, fasting, holiness, clothes, methods, walks, and denominations are offered as natural things that we can see, touch, and taste, which will make us spiritual, if we just do them. Yet, if you would just stop and look inside, you will see that there is no life coming out of you causing you to do these things. In other words, you are doing them not because you are spiritual, but you are doing them to become spiritual. It will not work. It is the same lie the devil told Eve. Eat and you shall be as gods. Just like Eve, when you do eat, you do become a god and strut around in your own righteousness, but you are a god who will die. You do not have the power to live.

You find the most cherished doctrines people hold to be those with the least chance of affecting the world they live in. Jesus spent His time going about doing good (Acts 10:38). He made a great impact on His world. But is that what most of Christianity is about? Isn't most of our time spent dividing, sub-dividing, theorizing, dissecting, and categorizing with little direct meaning for our lives? Who really wants to know whether the ancient Egyptians ate starfish or not? How much are your five points of Calvinism really going to benefit mankind? Does life really depend on pre- or post-millenniums? Just because you can say "per se" in Sunday school class, will that really benefit your family or the world you live in? Will your day really be made better having now heard the verb tense of that Greek word? How much are the heathen helped by your vow of poverty? Does your hour a day in prayer and frequent fasting bless and benefit those around you? And then if you really want to know the subtleties of it all, you have to actually belong to some group to appreciate the meaning of the words *independent, conservative, liberal, ultra-liberal, ultra-conservative.* How much do you really think this supports a spiritual life?

This deception goes to the heart of who has taught and is teaching the Church what she knows. Satan is more than glad for the opportunity to teach us that spirituality begins with the things that we see, hear, and taste. It is a frightening possibility that much of what is known in the Church is more hell-taught than heaven-birthed.

Paul dealt with this extensively. He said in Galatians 4:8–10, *"You did service to them which by nature are no gods. You have now turned back to them after you have known God, these weak and beggarly elements. You observe days, and months, and times, and years."*

To approach spirituality from the natural is to give service to the natural as though it were a god that could lead us higher. So, as the apostle says, we turn days and months and times and years into a god that we look to, to make us spiritual. The natural is a weak and beggarly element and can never lead us to life.

Will it then be a tree of life for our lives where living we may eat or a tree of knowledge where we eat but have no power to be? The hosts of heaven did not rejoice in the Garden when flesh became spiritual. They rejoiced that night when Spirit became flesh and Jesus was born. May God show us the difference.

There Is Order in Heaven

9

God is a God of order, and without order and authority bread making is hindered. There is a right way to do things. God is not order in the sense He is love, but He is the author of order. Order was not instituted because of sin, but was contained in God before the fall of man. Genesis 1:2: "The earth was without form and void and darkness was upon the deep. And the spirit of God moved upon the face of the waters." Coming upon a place of disorder and chaos, the Spirit of God did not leave such a condition but established order. After the fall of Adam the result was the same, the establishment of order. This context is important because of our tendency to associate the beginnings of order with sin and punishment. Order is not punishment to mankind but God's way of doing things.

To find order is not necessarily to find God, because there always will be imitators, but to find God is certainly to find order. Scripture tells us in Luke 3:4 that preparations for the Messiah would bring things into order that He might come. "Prepare ye the way of the LORD, make his paths straight, Every valley shall be filled and every mountain and hill shall be brought low; and the crooked shall be made straight, and the rough ways shall be made smooth" (Isa. 40:3–4). This scripture does not say life can come when there is a tingling in your spine, a whisper on the wind, or a voice in your dreams, but only when the very order of your world is changed.

Order is not deity, but is used by deity for expression. The existence of any order is dependant upon its usefulness to the expression of deity. God wills and does what He will at a moment's notice, and sometimes without a moment's notice; He will tear down, change, and replace a given form or order in exchange for another form or order—this all without regard to its dearness, preciousness, or length of tradition, for order is not God, but is used by God. Order directs life in the way God would have it flow, and if we block the flow God can and will make another orderly way, for life is never expressed through disorder.

> "God is not the author of confusion, but of peace, as in all the churches." (1 Cor. 14:33)

Your idea of order may not be God's idea, but He is a God of order. For the caterpillar to become a butterfly, he must have his cocoon. Without the cocoon, how can the worm become a butterfly? The cocoon, therefore, has value, and is in fact very necessary, but its value is completely connected with how well it cradles or holds life. Give the cocoon more value than that and it will refuse to break up and release the butterfly, killing instead of giving life. This is the state of organization in many churches today. They do not serve life but serve themselves.

The corn does not grow without the husk, but the husk can grow without the corn. Who has seen a healthy ear of corn without a healthy husk? But there are husks without corn, both in the field and in the Church. The form is there for the expression of life. The day the form becomes an end in itself is the day death begins. The day we no longer allow the reputation, good name, health, well being, and honor of our form to be used to further the gospel is the day we become just another religious organization.

NATURAL AND SPIRITUAL AUTHORITY

There are two realms of authority—natural and spiritual. Each has a distinct beginning and each continues as it began. The natural authority, though it affects the spiritual, will always be natural. The spiritual authority, though it affects the natural, will always be spiritual. So when one attempts to cross into the realm of the other by means other than effect, trouble occurs.

For example, earthly governments are part of the natural realm and should not seek to exercise spiritual authority. Romans 13:1 deals with the rightful order of earthly governments whose rulers operate in natural authority. Such rulers are a great blessing to those who do good works. In other words, they have an effect upon the spiritual atmosphere of the country when operating in their natural authority. Earthly governments are to apprehend evil doers, punish criminals, and maintain law and order, among other things. Such governments are no terror to good citizens. But in reality, many earthly governments indeed are a terror to good citizens, for they cross over from natural authority to spiritual authority. When governments use taxes, not just to raise operating money, but to punish rich people they believe have too much, giving it to those they believe need more, they are making spiritual judgments that no government is qualified to make. In extreme cases, governments such as Hitler's make judgments on who should live—whether older people, mentally handicapped, or certain races. Religious persecution comes when earthly governments support a certain church or spiritual belief with the force of arms. Only governments that cross over into spiritual authority become a terror to good people.

Romans 13:1 doesn't address this crossover and deals only with the original intent of earthly governments.

THE CHURCH

The authority of the Church, the Body of Christ, is spiritual. Though it does affect the natural, it is in its source spiritual. There must then be no attempt to cross over from spiritual authority into natural authority.

Examples of the effects of spiritual authority are many. When the apostle Peter, in Acts 5 spoke judgment against Ananias and Sapphira, he affected the natural without using natural force. Jesus healed all manner of disease and sickness (Matt. 10:1) without using any natural methods. The disciples were told in John 20:23, "Whosoever sins ye remit, they are remitted unto them; and whosesoever sins ye retain, they are retained." Such is spiritual authority. Its power affects the natural but does not use the natural. Force, coercion, threatening, or killing with the sword or tongue are not found in one who has spiritual authority. The reason the Church has lost its power is that its people have lost spiritual authority.

Much Church government is not really spiritual government, but earthly government revolving around a culture, interpretation, personality, or other visible religious manifestation. This Church government, which is really earthly government at heart, seeks to robe itself with spiritual authority backed up by the force of earthly authority.

Men and women are forced to obey by rules and regulations a standard of natural righteousness. Leaders use threats and coercion just as earthly governments do to get their followers to obey. Psychology is used quite liberally in the Church in our times—in marriage counseling, in Church relationships, in personal counseling, and in the general form and structure of the Church. There was a day when the Church did not look to the world for its authority.

The Church has always had its means of dealing with the moral corruption of any generation without itself operating out of the power of that generation. But a church with only natural authority must use natural force and laws to implement righteousness. Jesus and the apostles never marched in the streets against the moral evils of their day or picketed the establishments of evil men. They never lent the hand of the Church to passing laws for general morality and virtue. The Church affected those laws, but the world to them was the world, and the Church to them was quite another thing. They preached a gospel that changed their own lives and the lives of those with them.

By contrast, the Church today produces results that speak for themselves, as surveys of Christian people are out there for all to see. The percentage of Church people in fornication, adultery, divorce, abortion, and a long string of other sins is just as high, if not higher, than that of the general population. This is not the record of a church operating in spiritual authority.

PREACHING JESUS WITHOUT A BODY

1 John 4:1–3: "Beloved, believe not every spirit, but try the spirits whether they are of God: because many false prophets are gone out into the world. Hereby know ye the Spirit of God: Every spirit that confesseth that Jesus Christ is come in

the flesh is of God: And every spirit that confesseth not that Jesus Christ is come in the flesh is not of God: and this is that spirit of antichrist, whereof ye have heard that it should come; and even now already is it in the world."

According to this Scripture, a spirit has gone out into this world that speaks of spiritual life without a physical body. We all know, no doubt, that God is a spirit and so exists as a pure spirit and undefiled. That is not what this false spirit is referring to. It teaches a spiritual Jesus only. It already has so exposed us to its teachings that we are a little startled at the thought of putting the spiritual on equal footing with the natural. But that's what we must do. When Jesus became a man, His flesh was just as much God as was His spirit. That is not to say that we can turn the Incarnation around and claim that man becomes God. We are not permitted at this time to move from the natural to the spiritual, only from the spiritual to the natural. It is the occult that claims that man can become a god. It is heaven that tells us that God became a man. We need to proclaim that God became a man, because when that happened, it so shook the very foundations of the fallen spirit world that since then no devil will confess that Jesus came in the flesh. For a devil to do so would be to admit his own defeat. Any preaching that acknowledges a spiritual Jesus only is in error and is knowingly or unknowingly following false spirits.

These false spirits, even in the Church, use phrases with double meanings—meanings that taken the right way would be true, but taken with a second, implied, meaning become quite wrong. Often these phrases are used to get past our guard and plant false doctrine.

Jesus Only

One such phrase is "I preach only Jesus." No one wants to resist anything so pure that it has only Jesus in it. This

Jesus being taught, though, is usually only a spiritual Jesus. And again we already want to think, "Well, the more spiritual the better." No, more spiritual is not better if it excludes the flesh. Jesus is not just spiritual anymore, for He has come in the flesh. Now that He is gone back to heaven, Jesus still has His body, and any work He does on this earth is done through spirit and body. What does this all mean?

In its simplest form, perhaps, we can see what it means in the Sermon on the Mount, as found in Matthew 5, 6, and 7. When Jesus spoke to the people, He referred to things they used and could relate to—things such as salt, a candle, a bushel, a city set on a hill, lilies in the field, fowls of the air, fish, trees that could bear only one kind of fruit, rain that falls from the skies, and floods that rise. Perhaps the significance of these natural things has never dawned on us because of how accustomed we are to reading them. But this kind of teaching was not acceptable in the religious synagogue of that day. No self-respecting rabbi would ever speak of trees, flowers, and birds in his message to the people. Why not? Because these belong to the natural world, and he, the rabbi, was spiritual. He could never lower himself to a natural level. Yet Jesus did just that. He spoke of the natural, and not only spoke of it, but connected it to the spiritual. From a candle Jesus drew spiritual lessons, and from flowers He taught us of great spiritual things. So well has this been hidden in Christianity that few understand what Jesus really did. The divide He crossed indeed is great, and only the spiritual man can apprehend it. Many who are acting spiritual are really natural and cannot believe in real spirituality.

Since Jesus has come in the flesh, we must beware of a man who teaches an only-spiritual doctrine or claims to be himself only spiritual. Such teaching suggests demonic influence. It is easy to present ourselves as above the fray and free from the struggles of everyday man, but it is hard to be honest and walk like a true man. This is the great argument. Can the spiritual be natural? Can I sleep as other men and still be spiritual, or must I to be spiritual pretend that I stay awake every night all night praying? Can I eat as other men and be spiritual, or must I be spiritual and fast as the Pharisees did, twice a week, and pretend that I am doing it a lot more? Can spirituality be a normal man, or must we be unlike the way God made us to be spiritual?

Or the question can be asked from the other angle. Is your spirituality really spiritual? Are you actually as spiritual as you are pretending to be? After your fasting and praying, are you now spiritual? When Jesus put this question to some men who thought they were holy, standing around a woman caught in adultery with stones in their hands, none of them could answer with a *yes* (John 8:7). They all had to walk away with eyes to the ground. These religious men thought they were much more spiritual than Jesus who talked of birds, flowers, and trees in His sermons. Yet when it came time to produce fruit, the "spiritual" people had no fruit, but the Man who was so natural in their eyes had much fruit. So who do we think was really spiritual?

To preach only Jesus is correct if the Jesus you are preaching is a man. The flesh that Christ came in was not something other—it was He. So now also, Jesus is not just spirit but also a body. So are His people, the Church. They are not only spiritual, but also men and women.

Jesus gave us a test of spirituality: "By their fruits ye shall know them" (Matt. 7:20). Fruit, in its basic element, is natural. Go taste an apple or orange if you do not believe this. Of course fruit also can be applied in a spiritual sense, but the basic meaning as Jesus used it was very natural. We would do well not to forget that. So the question is again, are you what you say you are? Or are you a spiritual giant in church but with no fruit, nothing natural, to show for it? For all your praying, are there people around you who are the better for it? Or do they just admire you as a spiritual man? For all your church going and attendance at meetings, is your family the better for it and closer drawn together? Does your spirituality have fruit, or is it just spiritual?

The body Jesus walked in while on this earth had a culture, a language, and a people He was born into. All this was not something added, as if separate from Him. They were His own. John 1:11 says, "He came unto his own, and his own received him not." As men and women—and as Christians—we belong to a culture, a language, a family, and a way of life. They are not to be made special or superior one over the other, but they also are not to be denied as nonexistent. Many people who present themselves as spiritual say they are above these things and have none of them. If they say that, they are saying they are not like Jesus and are more spiritual than He was.

The apostle Paul dealt with this in 1 Corinthians 1:12, where he speaks of those who say they are of Paul, of Apollos, and of Cephas, and then Paul adds "of Christ" to the list. Here we see both errors—one of making one man special over the other, and the other of making everything spiritual. We still have both errors with us today. Some make one man special, and some say they are only spiritual and follow no man, just a spiritual Jesus.

He Just Taught Me

Another phrase often used along these lines is, "Someone has just taught you that." The idea is to avoid human involvement in what you know, because if it has come through a human, it cannot be as pure as if you got it straight from the Spirit. This kind of thinking is a recipe for demonic activity. It is not that we don't receive revelations, dreams, and such directly from the Spirit—that is not the point. The point is, from where and through what means is the teaching coming? Does a teaching coming through a man dilute it, as the one side says, or is a teaching coming through a man a safeguard against false teaching? Sadly, many Christians prefer to be taught directly by dreams and revelations or directly from another man's dream or revelation, rather than be taught by a man who has had a dream or revelation. The difference is important and great.

Jesus did not use His supernatural experiences to directly teach the people. There is no record that I know of in Scripture of Jesus calling up front someone who was healed to give his testimony. I read nothing of the blind who were healed and the lepers who were cleansed being placed in newsletter reports for whatever reason. When Jesus came up out of the water after His baptism, a voice spoke out of heaven saying, "This is my Beloved Son in whom I am well pleased" (Matt. 3:17). There is no record of Jesus ever teaching out of that experience. He did not open His sermons with, "A voice spoke to Me out of heaven and said that God is well pleased with Me. So you all listen to Me and make no trouble for Me." That is not what He did. Jesus opened His mouth and taught the people without any reference to any supernatural experience.

Another time a voice spoke to Him out of heaven and some who stood by said it thundered. Jesus did not correct that misunderstanding as some preachers would today in order to get the full benefit of the experience. Jesus did say that the voice spoke for the people's sake, but He did not teach out of it (John 12:28–30).

On the Mount of Transfiguration with three of His disciples, Jesus was glorified in white garments and spoke with Moses and Elias. As was usual with Jesus, upon coming down from the mountain He told the disciples to "tell the vision to no man" (Matt. 17:1–9). But the Scriptures say Jesus, when He taught, simply opened His mouth and taught the people (Matt. 5:2).

The apostle Paul did recount his conversion experience, but was forbidden to speak of his experiences in the third heavens. In 2 Corinthians 12:4, Paul says that the words he heard in paradise are unspeakable words. Today, with revelations in hand, that would be the first thing some preachers would talk about. And considering that the words Paul heard in paradise were unspeakable, it makes you wonder where those preachers get theirs. The apostle, without speaking of those things he had seen, wrote Scriptures, blessing and changing the world even now some two thousand years later, while modern day preachers talking all about their great revelations do little but deceive.

The apostle Peter in Acts 10 received a revelation from God concerning the Gentiles. Peter first acted out the instructions before he told anyone the account of his dream. We, on the contrary, would probably come down from the upstairs room where we had our dream and immediately say, "Ah, let me tell you what just happened to me." We would tell everyone in the room everything that had happened and then head on down to Joppa and wonder why things did not turn out well. Peter did not do that. Although later he told the story, he first acted out the instructions of the dream, and he never taught out of the dream. There is a difference, and we would do well to learn it.

It is true that just because we are taught something from parents, leaders, teachers, or whomever does not mean that it must be true. The issue we are dealing with is people who are unable to hear sound advice and instruction given to them by authority figures simply on the basis that they are human. These same people go home and think the most unusual, wild, unsound, and unholy thoughts and believe them to be true because they see no man attached to them. No doubt some of these thoughts are their own, but many of them could well be the work of demon spirits. Many unsuspecting souls by such false concepts have been rendered open to deceiving thoughts and spirits, simply on the basis that these things must be good because they are only spiritual and unrobed in flesh.

WHAT OF CULTURE?

Then there is the whole issue of culture. Are spiritual Christians really culture-less, as is sometimes implied? It is true that culture has no special significance in spiritual things, nor is one superior to the other as religion sometimes makes them. Yet, does the gospel come without culture? If you were really free in Christ, would you have no culture?

The answer is quite simple, as one needs only ask whether Jesus had a culture. He did, of course, and by having one Jesus did not elevate that culture above any other. He just had one, like you and I have one. Culture means little in its natural state, nor does it mean much more once a new creature in Christ is birthed into that culture, other than that culture belongs to that new creature. It is his own and so obtains significance only on that basis.

The wisest and most successful missionaries are those who do not attempt to change the weaknesses in the cultures of the heathen they minister to, but simply preach the gospel, letting it have its effect upon the culture. Many success stories in organizations such as New Tribes Mission could make the point. Others, however, take their own culture overseas and, thinking it superior or part of the gospel, impose it upon the local natives. The resulting damage is there for anyone who wants to see, from the inferiority complexes of the natives, to their stunted growth in spiritual matters.

Spiritual and natural things are in Christ at peace with one another. It is useless for the Church in its search for spirituality to attempt to obliterate cultures, nationalities, races, and the roles of men and women. In Christ there is neither male nor female nor Jew nor Greek, but we don't arrive at such a state by obliterating the natural states. The world says that men and women are equal. The Bible says so also, but the two mean quite different things by what they say. To the world being equal means ceasing to be men and women and becoming the same. In the Scriptures, being equal means fully developing into men and women without the resulting differences affecting their mutual value, peace, and equality.

Galatians 3:28: "*There is neither Jew nor Greek, there is neither bond nor free, there is neither male nor female: for ye are all one in Christ Jesus.*" Paul never meant to obliterate such states as the Jew and Greek, the slave and free, and the male and female. The world can try to do that. What he meant was something much greater—that without changing their natural states the natural states would cease to matter. Even the world can make two things that are the same agree, but only God can make two things that are different agree. That is why the more we become one with God, the more we become like ourselves; and also the more we love each other, the more different we become. Our salvation is not a little salvation but a great salvation. Most preachers do not dream too large dreams but live too small lives.

The world is busy trying to obtain oneness by making everyone the same. The world needs everyone to be the same so it can get its work done. God does not work with such feeble power. The natural in its created state as God made it is no hindrance to the power and workings of God. It is a hindrance only to the working of evil. In God, true individuality is established, not undone. God wants there to be different cultures, languages, peoples, races, and customs in this world for the very precise reason that these are hindrances and roadblocks to evil. From the tower of Babel onward it has been so. These hindrances that God put in place when He divided up the human race by confounding its languages do not hinder the gospel, but they do hinder the spread of evil and false doctrine. Error must have sameness in order to function well and will always seek to obliterate these hindrances and override them, while the gospel does neither. One needs only to listen to the talk of one-world-government and one-world-religion to see how much the world desires sameness. Evil wishes for things to be like they were before the tower of Babel. But we need not look out at the large picture of the world to see all this. A close look around our own homes will no doubt show the encroachment of this spirit of sameness into our lives. This spirit says we all are spiritual and do not have different ways of doing things, when Scripture says we do (1 Cor. 12:4–7). Gone then is the need for tolerance, love, and peacemaking, and with it the real power of the gospel. It takes no special virtue to run in a herd, but it takes the Spirit of God to love my neighbor who is a Samaritan to me.

The Role of the Natural

10

We can not make bread if we are so spiritual that the natural does not affect us. True, the life from the natural is not used by God, but the natural is used by the enduing of new life. Roman 12:2: *"Be ye transformed by the renewing of your mind."* What this means is that God doesn't want us to think on our own, but He does want us to think. We are not to sit around and think, scheme, and plan by ourselves, but we are to use our minds, even when filled with the Spirit of God. Maybe this sounds like an unnecessary thing to say, and maybe it would be if there were not preachers who were trying to get you to stop thinking and just accept what they tell you. Just because I am not to think by my own power does not mean that I am not to think at all when filled with the Spirit.

Following the Spirit is not flowing with the wind. John 3:8 does not say that the Spirit of God is as the wind. It says the one who is born of the Spirit is as the wind. He who follows the Spirit looks to the surrounding world as mysterious as the wind, but the one born of the Spirit is not following the wind. There is a difference.

When the work of God is done in the natural, there will still be the form, structure, and body. That means that after I am a Christian I will still think. We are instructed to be that way because it inconveniences those who try to teach us false doctrine. Most false teachers try to stop their followers from thinking. The Spirit of God does not. That is because the Spirit of God has power and is not hindered by our thinking. The false teacher is weak and must remove our thinking for him to work. There are places in Christian circles where in prayer lines people are told to quit praying so that they can receive the blessing. There are places where a blank mind is considered necessary for the flowing of the spirit. There are places where those who think and ask questions are told to do what they are told. This is not Christianity as defined by Jesus.

To deny oneself is not to deny who we are in our basic created form, but to deny the rights, privileges, and life that the natural brings with it. Such is dying in the scriptural sense. Obliteration is the enemy's interpretation of dying, and brings a death from which there is no awakening.

Jesus Came in the Flesh

The concept of God coming in the flesh is one of great embarrassment to all the fallen worlds. False spirits will always work against that concept, because it drives at the heart of what they have become and what heaven is. All the workings of evil were undone and the heart of the matter exposed when a Man from heaven died on the cross. For heaven has life in itself and is not afraid to be left alone in the flesh. There is no need in heaven of bluster or show, for life is contained in God Himself. Heaven has great confidence in life. It is believers without life and confidence in life who must walk a path unhindered from the flesh. If the Church has life, then the Greek, the Jew, the bond, the free, the male, and the female, staying in their respective places, do not hinder the advance of the Church. If the Church has not life, it must obliterate the differences for advancement to occur. The apostle Paul never said the Jew must lay aside his identity for him to reach the Jew or that the Greek must lay aside his identity for him to reach the Greek. What the apostle said was, *"And unto the Jews I became as a Jew, that I might gain the Jews; to them that are under the law, as under the law, that I might gain them that are under the law; To them that are without law, as without law, (being not without law to God, but under the law to Christ,) that I might gain them that are without law. To the weak became I as weak, that I might gain the weak: I am made all things to all men, that I might by all means save some"* (1 Cor. 9:20–22).

By this Paul did not mean that he watered down the gospel to fit the situation, but that he himself made all things his own. Such is the power of the gospel, that this did not hinder or dilute the gospel itself. Evil cannot do this, for it has not life in itself. Life will burst forth where it is planted. The grave could not hold Life. Death could not stop Life. The problem of the Church is the lack of Life, and our constant fear of outward hindrances bears record of it.

THE STRIPPING DOWN

The ultimate expression of God becoming flesh was Christ dying upon the cross. We need the perspective of the spirit world to understand this. To become flesh is to strip down spiritual powers. That means that God, to become a man, had to become weak like we are. His power was stripped down. God as a spirit does not sleep, but God as a man did. God is so great in power that He could accept sleeping and not lose any of His power. False spirits cannot accept this, because they are weak. If they slept, something might steal away their power and authority.

Jesus is so great in power and authority that He could accept the limitations of a man and not cease to be God. There were times He had to ask questions as when, in the middle of a crowd, He did not see who had touched Him and asked, "Who touched me?" (Luke 8:45). Jesus was willing to accept not always knowing everything, because that did not affect His power. False spirits cannot accept this and always have to know everything. We should be careful about leaders who want to know everything we are doing all the time. It is a mark of weakness. Jesus was willing to accept not knowing everything.

Philippians 2:5–8: *"Let this mind be in you, which was also in Christ Jesus: Who, being in the form of God, thought it not robbery to be equal with God: But made himself of no reputation, and took upon him the form of a servant, and was made in the likeness of men: And being found in fashion as a man, he humbled himself, and became obedient unto death, even the death of the cross."*

This mind that was in Christ Jesus will be in those who are born of Him. Jesus was not afraid to be weak in the flesh, because He was strong in the Spirit. He laid the demonic world and fallen spirits to an open shame as He walked in this world.

The Question of Life

At the root of Christ's humanity lies the question of life. Jesus could become weak because He had life in Himself. Life is strength, so the man who has life can accept weakness and still be strong. A man who has no life must reject weakness because he has no life to bear him up in weakness. Taboos and restrictions are placed by religion to keep men away from weakness, so that they can at least appear to have strength. The apostle Paul said we are to receive such people who are weak in faith but not to give their arguments grounds by disputing with them (Rom. 14:1). It is strange to us that weakness, and not strength, should involve things like abstaining from meats or drinks and respecting holy days, new moons, and Sabbath days (Col. 2:16). Spiritual strength is to walk weak in the flesh. This the Son of God Himself clearly demonstrated when He took on human weakness, showing that He had life.

Jesus made Himself of no reputation and became a servant to all without losing any of His deity. This is a daily reminder to this day that life is self-sustaining and self-existing. To become weak from the view of spirit beings is to erect roadblocks or hindrances in one's life. The fallen spirits can have no hindrances or even acknowledge a life that can exist in hindrances, for that would expose the death they contain within themselves.

Christ did not simply robe Himself in human flesh; He *became* that flesh. He became tired and remedied the problem, not by some spiritual manifestation, but by sleeping. That is submitting to limitation. When Christ desired to travel from Judea to Galilee, He walked or rode, not by spiritual powers, but on a donkey, perhaps, or by His own two feet. That is submitting to limitation. Christ limited Himself primarily to one race and group of people, the Jews. That is limitation. Christ lived and died perhaps thirty to forty miles from where He was born, submitted to circumcision, to baptism, to His parents, to a job, to tools of His trade, and to the identity of a Jew. None of these restrictions in any way diminished, diluted, watered-down, or restrained His message, His gospel, or His life. Today there is no corner of the earth where His gospel cannot go.

For any man to come even close to walking in this truth is for him to invite ridicule, mockery, and insults against his manhood and validity as a Christian.

No false spirits when teaching what they believe will confess to this truth, for to do so is to confess to the lie that they themselves embody. False doctrine has as its basic modus operandi the removal of weakness contained in cultures, teachings, methods, forms, and structures. That's the only way it can propagate itself. The gospel of Christ does not operate this way but calls all to repentance. Repentance is not obliteration of the basic culture, form, or structure. It is the introduction and acceptance of another life that can walk holy where the weak flesh of every man walks.

The Life Which Is No Life

There is a life that is not really living. Maybe that sounds strange, but I believe it to be true. Those who avoid weakness as a way of defining their own strength have this problem: they make their own strength dependent upon the existence of weakness. A man who fasts twice a week as the Pharisee did in Matthew 18:12 must define that strength by a man who does not fast twice a week. He is defining his strength by another's weakness. If everyone fasted there would be no way of defining fasting twice a week as a spiritual strength. Therefore, fasting twice a week, which looks like a strength, cannot stand on it own. It must have a weakness to make it strong.

A man known as a praying man because we frequently see him go up to prayer must have a weakness present—a man who does not go up to pray—for his praying to be considered a strength. For going up to prayer to be considered a strength, there must be men who do not pray. If there are men present who pray more, the praying, which was a strength, becomes a weakness. So the man who does not pray and who is weak is more like God than the one who looks strong, because weakness is self-contained and self-existent.

This is how foolish some of our strengths look to God. They are a life, but they are not really living. Paul spoke of this life that is not really life in 1 Timothy 5:16 when he referred to one who was dead while she lived. Life to be life must be self-sustaining and existent. That is why God uses weakness and not strength as the ultimate expression of His power. It is because weakness can stand alone. It is self-defining. A broken leg is still a broken leg, no matter how many strong legs there are in the world or how many worse broken legs, but a strong leg becomes a weak leg if there are other legs stronger than itself.

So we have those concluding verses of 1 Corinthians chapter 1 in which Paul says, *"God has chosen the foolish things of the world to confound the wise; and God hath chosen the weak things of the world to confound the things which are mighty. And base things of the world and things which are despised, hath God chosen, yea, and things which are not, to bring to naught things that are."* God told Paul in 2 Corinthians 12:9 that His strength was made perfect in weakness.

The same holds true for disorder and error. Neither can exist on its own. Disorder could not even define itself in the absence of order. Neither can something be wrong unless there is something right. While on the other hand, order and truth exist on their own. We would not know it was dark if there had never been light, but we would know of light, even if there were no darkness. People long ago thought the earth was flat. They were wrong, but they could not have been wrong if the earth had not been made round. If I believe birds fly, I am right, even though no one thinks they crawl on their stomachs. If I believe that birds crawl on their stomachs, I cannot be wrong unless birds fly. Truth stands alone, error does not. The same is true of disorder. How would we know that an egg is broken unless we compared it to the way hens lay them? But when the hens lay them, you do not need a cracked egg to know that this egg is normal.

This logic on truth and error of course leads us to quite a frightening conclusion perhaps, and it is this. Does error in the absence of truth become the truth? Did not people once believe the earth was flat? Is a cracked egg normal if you have no whole egg to compare it with? The answer by some convoluted way is yes. Deceived people do think they are right; otherwise, how are they deceived. It is truth though with a severe identity problem. Error masquerading as the truth is a restless thing. It walks around looking for something to be against, or it insists on isolation from all opposing views. Error wakes up every morning in doubt and must prove each day that it is right. It is my belief that God will break through to every man or woman that is in error. At some time or place on this earth the attempt will be made to reach them. The choice will be up to the individual then whether he will love the truth with all its cold and hard reality, or continue with the ease of the lie.

Disorder and error look strong because they destroy order and truth, but they are themselves not strong but must feed off of something else to exist. We should be encouraged by the presence of error and disorder, as they bear testimony, although unwillingly, to the existence of truth and order. The apostle Paul took this attitude in 1 Corinthians 11: 19 when he said, *"there must be also heresies among you, that they which are approved may be made manifest."* I am not sure my feelings agree with that, as we are usually troubled by the presence of error and wrong.

Do we not also often cast around eagerly for some way of getting rid of this flesh, our weakness, by which we mean the way we are, our culture, our way of life, and our upbringing? We sigh to be more spiritual, hardly being aware of what we say.

What about Prayer and Fasting
The question will no doubt then be asked: if prayer, fasting, and such things are really often practiced as weaknesses, are we then not to do them, or at least very little? Jesus told us how to do these things. We are to do them in secret—that is, to practice them as a weakness. Only then are they a strength.

If we fast we are to wash our face and put on deodorant as usual so we look as if we are not fasting (Matt. 6:17). Why is this? So we look weak even when we are operating in a strength.

If we give alms we are not to let our right hand know what the left is doing (Matt. 6:3). Why is this? It is so we stay in weakness, even when walking in a strength. Not giving alms is weak, and even when we give alms we are to stay in weakness. Because that is where God will meet us.

If we pray, we are to shut the door and enter our closet, and there pray in secret, or in weakness, so God will meet us because He will meet us in our weakness (Matt. 6:6). We have to ask ourselves, how Christian really are we?

Righteous Justice

Many people focus upon what they call "the moving of the Spirit." They operate under the fear of quenching the Spirit, by which they mean hindering or judging anything that is spiritually expressed. This is a valid concern and should not be brushed aside lightly; but just because something is spiritual does not automatically make it right, nor make it unnecessary to judge. There is a judging that is scriptural and a judging that is carnal. There is a quenching, Scripture says, that is not to be done. 1 Thessalonians 5:19: "*Quench not the Spirit.*" I doubt if there is much use having a discussion over what can or cannot be judged or should be judged. It seems to me from a reading of 1 Corinthians 14, verse 29 in particular, that judging as defined by Scripture is an expected part of any Christian activity. This doesn't involve a critical attitude but a constant watch for evil, as a shepherd would watch the woods for the wolves. It is not that the shepherd is critical of the woods, but they do produce wolves that kill his sheep.

If there is spiritual activity going on that cannot tolerate this watchfulness, then one has to question the validity of such a spirituality. It appears to me also from the apostle Paul's remarks to the Bereans that he had no problem with people who asked questions. Acts 17:11: "*These searched the scriptures daily, whether those things were so.*" The gospel seems to have no problem operating in an environment of searching. Scriptural judging does not extinguish except what it is supposed to extinguish.

John 7:24: "*Judge not according to the appearance, but judge righteous judgment.*"

Spiritual expression that cannot survive hindrance or righteous judging is fundamentally flawed and weak. Any church is on dangerous ground that operates in tongues, tears, prophesies, dreams, visions, laying on of hands, and other spiritual things without judgment.

Moving in the Flesh

Then there are people of religious persuasion who make their start from the outside in. They do not have a high opinion of questions. Here the natural is held as sacred spiritual ground and not tongues, dreams, and visions. One is no less a spirituality to them than the other. Their spirituality in the natural consists of clothes, observances of days, prayer time, fasting, giving money, not eating meat, and such things.

The rationale for emphasizing these things is our intuitive understanding that inward spiritual things ought to show up outside. Is not the dislike for hypocrites universal? It seems to me that it is. A hypocrite is someone who does not practice what he preaches. So people know that what a person says he ought to do. This knowledge is, I believe, in the hearts of all people.

The appeal is then made to this knowledge on two levels. First, since the human heart knows that the invisible ought to be visible, the visible is presented as evidence that the invisible is already in place. They have a problem, though, in that the visible as God made it is quite natural and does not attract much attention. For example, praying and crying aloud to God on a passenger train about to collide would not be considered very unusual or much worthy of credit by anyone riding on the train. If you want to be noticed as spiritual by praying on a train, you have to do it in an unnatural manner to attract attention.

Take clothes as another example. If clothes that are usual to the culture are worn in a manner that do what clothes are supposed to do—cover the body—that does not attract much attention by anyone. If you want to attract attention with your clothes so they look spiritual, you have to wear something unnatural. Simple modesty is not unnatural. What is unnatural is a distinct style or pattern that makes a religious statement or an over-exaggerated form of modesty. A kind of visible righteousness that comes from a normal spiritual life is not sufficient or satisfactory.

All religious expressions are unnatural. Whether through prayer, clothing, fasting, or in the keeping of days, they are exaggerated versions of natural spiritual inclinations put in us by God. We all have the natural inclination to cover our bodies. When we follow that inclination it produces nothing all that unusual. It is the man on the street without a shirt on that catches my eye, not the one with one on. There is another way to catch my eye, though, and that is to wear a religious shirt. That is as unnatural as not wearing a shirt.

In this way an outward expression is produced that can be worshiped, causing men to retain traditions and doctrines that never had usefulness in the kingdom of God. Order must be useful to be part of the kingdom. To honor outward expressions for their own sakes is to worship them. The world stands in admiration of much of religious expression. The apostle warns of a worship of the creature more than the Creator (Rom. 1:23). We always thought this was just the heathen dancing in the jungle around his idol that looked like an animal. But these inclinations of God to pray and clothe ourselves are just as much His creation as anything is. If we end up worshiping forms of them, we are no better than the savage in the jungle. For out of this worship comes, as Romans 1:28–29 says: *"And even as they did not like to retain God in their knowledge, God gave them over to a reprobate mind, to do those things which are not convenient; Being filled with all unrighteousness, fornication, wickedness, covetousness, maliciousness; full of envy, murder, debate, deceit, malignity; whisperers."*

There must be righteous judgment of spirituality, whether it is natural or spiritual.

The Church

The believer will always be tested. The believers of the past have been tested in the extreme—with the kingdoms of this world, with the mouths of lions, with the violence of fire, with weakness, in fight with the armies of aliens, with death, with tortures, with trials of cruel mockings and scourgings, with bonds and imprisonments (Heb. 11:33–37). Put a Paul in prison, let all Asia forsake him, and he writes most of the New Testament. Put a John Bunyan in prison for twelve-plus years and he writes *Pilgrim's Progress*. These are men and women of whom the world is not worthy (Heb. 11:38). This is the life of the Church. Restrict it, prune it, cut it back, and it grows but greater and bears more fruit.

EXAGGERATIONS AND RELIGIOUS EXPRESSIONS

A terrible union between the sons of God and the daughters of men produced children who were giants of old. Genesis 6:4: "There were giants in the earth in those days; and also after that, when the sons of God came in unto the daughters of men, and they bare children to them, the same became mighty men which were of old, men of renown."

When evil plays a part in making a man the result is not a normal human being as in the birth of Jesus, but the creation of giants. Giants are an exaggerated form of humanity. Using computations of modern science, any human being loses his normality in function somewhere between seven and eight feet of height because of the body's inability to support the resulting weight (*The Genesis Question*, Hugh Ross, NavPress, 1998). He concludes that giants could not have functioned as they did in battle without some form of demonic influence upon their body structure.

We are given the measurements of giants in 2 Samuel 21:15–22 and 1 Chronicles 20:5–8. Goliath was nine feet, nine inches tall. He demonstrated great mobility and strength in battle, carrying at least 250 pounds of armor and weapons. Og, the king of Bashan, had an iron bed to sleep in measuring thirteen-and-a-half by six feet. The enormous weight of weapons and armor carried by these giants, in addition to that of their own stature, supersedes human capabilities and the limits of normal biological engineering. The bone mass in humans necessary to support the muscles and resist the effects of gravity rises with height. This ratio means that any human being taller than eight feet loses a great amount of his freedom of movement and lacks the strength to carry the weights even of his own body. The tallest modern human on record was eight feet eleven inches tall. This man was unable to participate in sports and died at the age of forty from physical exhaustion. Basketball players lose their advantage of height somewhere between seven and seven-and-a-half feet. It would therefore seem to be a physical and biological impossibility that human beings could be as tall, move as fast, and carry as much weight as Goliath.

The conclusion, then, based on indications in Scripture, is that some degree of demonic influence or possession must have been involved in the exaggerated sizes of giants. Another fearful conclusion is that religious exaggerated forms of the natural also cannot be maintained without help from the wrong side.

We in the religious world would do well to heed the warning signs. Scripture calls things the doctrines of devils that we may not think worthy of the name. Two such doctrines are prohibitions against marriage and eating meat (1 Tim. 4:3). Both involve modifications of normal human behavior for religious reasons. Paul was not married at the time of his writing 1 Corinthians seven, and he spoke of instances where abstaining of meats was in order (Rom. 14:21), but he never attempted to modify normal God-given human behavior as a feature of Christianity. To modify and exaggerate is a mark of demonic influence upon the flesh.

To our shame, human beings have acquired a taste for exaggeration. Isaiah 53:3 speaks of the Son of God, that He would have no beauty that we should desire Him. This does not mean He would be ugly or disfigured. Our perception of His lack of beauty would stem from our love for the modified and the exaggerated. The Son of God came among us as a normal human being. This pulls and turns wrong in our souls, for we believe that greatness of spirit must translate into greatness of flesh. We wanted, if not a giant, a very remarkable human being. What a testament to our fallenness.

During Christ's three years of public ministry, people struggled to make sense of Him and connect the Man with what He did. Do we not know his brothers and his mother? they asked. And his sisters are they not with us? (Matt. 13:55–56). Their implication was this: He was never any different from us, so how does He do these miracles? They wanted to see an exaggerated man to match the great works Christ was doing. Jesus had no beauty that we should desire Him, because He was not fallen like we are. Jesus was robed in the simple beauty of heaven.

There is order in God and in His Church. It is simple, normal, peaceful, and it makes bread.

Acknowledgments

I want to thank Jon Marken from Lamp-Post Publicity for his editing of this book. He took my work and returned a readable version of the manuscript. His critique on the ordering and structure of the book were of great value to me.

Also, thanks to Chester Wright and John Martin who, so many years ago, supplied in sermons the starting point for my thought processes—Mr. Wright on the ancient structure of bread making and Mr. Martin on the yeast. Although neither of them knows me, the basic ideas in those two sections started from them with the thoughts and applications over the years being my own.

Index of Scriptures

All Scripture references given in which the prior text is not in quotation marks should be understood to mean that the text taken from the reference is not a direct quote.

Micah

6:6–8	112
6:8	55

Zechariah

9:9	80

Matthew

Matthew (continued)

23:15	60
23:25, 27	60
23:28	31, 71
23:33	60, 71
24:24–26	70
26:26	82
26:28	82

Mark

8:15	48, 50, 54
8:33	25
10:15	62
12:33	104
14:22	11
15:34	79
16:15	29

Luke

2:49–52	30
3:4	121
4:1–2	63
4:3	21
4:3–4	63
4:4	65
4:5–7	67
4:7	68
4:9–12	71
6:23	41
8:15	72
8:45	138
8:5	19
10:30–36	61
13:33	42
18:20	68
20:46	59
22:16	98
22:32	37
23:46	79

John

1 Corinthians (continued)

2 Corinthians

Galatians

Ephesians

Philippians

James

1 Peter

1 John

To order additional copies of

TRANSFORMING
the believer

Have your credit card ready and call

Toll free: (877) 421-READ (7323)

or send $10.95** each plus $4.95 S&H* to

WinePress Publishing
PO Box 428
Enumclaw, WA 98022

www.winepresspub.com

**WA residents, add 8.4% sales tax

*add $1.00 S&H for each additional book ordered

Published for Gospel for the World, Farmville, VA

Please visit our website:
www.gospelontheweb.com

Contact the author at jseicher@ceva.net